Creating Climate Wealth:

Unlocking the Impact Economy

Jigar Shah

Dedication:

This book is dedicated to my wife, Khushali Shah, who encouraged me to be the person I am today—one without hesitation or fear. It is also dedicated to my family, who instilled in me deep-seated lessons of integrity and humility, ones that stay with you when you are tested and ultimately challenged in ways you dream unthinkable.

Table of Contents

Section III: Putting $10 Trillion to Work

Foreword

This may seem strange, but before I ever knew Jigar Shah, I knew about the business model he developed and deployed for solar energy services company SunEdison. I was so excited about the business model when I first saw it; I posted it on Slideshare for all the world to see. Jigar was one of the people who saw my post; he contacted me, and it is how we connected. That was in 2007.

I actually did not meet Jigar in person until 2010 at a Carbon War Room event in London. So, between 2007 and 2010, we exchanged emails, phone calls, and more.

I was deeply intrigued when I first discovered SunEdison's business model based on power purchase agreements. I started to understand how powerful Jigar's model was by analyzing it with a tool I developed. It didn't surprise me that the company was on its way to being a key catalyst in growing solar energy services into a multibillion-dollar industry—and making SunEdison the largest solar services company in the world.

The most interesting aspect of SunEdison's business model, however, was that it provided more than just a business advantage; it also provided an advantage to society beyond economic stimulus and profits.

SunEdison's value proposition included the delivery of electricity to customers that was guaranteed to cost equal to, or less than, the utility rates each paid—and locked in that low rate for a long-term contract, usually twenty years. So there was economic value. But because the energy was solar, it was clean, reliable, and silent. So there was a social benefit: no carbon.

Today, I see unbelievable untapped wealth potential in entrepreneurial approaches where managers and entrepreneurs build business models that don't "just" seek to make a profit, but also seek to change the world in a scalable way.

I don't make the above statement lightly. Business models and innovations in large companies, start-ups, and nonprofits have been the focus of my work for more than a decade. One of the most exciting developments I have encountered is a steady rise of business models that actually do create (financial) wealth for the organizations and wealth for society at large. So it is profits plus—the plus is a positive and desirable impact on societal and environmental issues in general in addition to better, cheaper, or new products and services. I call these approaches "Business Models beyond Profit."

In these Business-Models-beyond-Profit businesses, profits and impact live in harmony. Jigar Shah's story of SunEdison is one of the world's great examples of this new harmonious relationship between profits and impact. SunEdison was not just a highly profitable and fast-growing company; it changed the face of the solar energy sector forever and helped the industry rise to new levels.

Unlocking Endless Opportunities

Opportunities to deliver a positive societal and environmental impact are almost unlimited. The reason? Almost everywhere we turn, we can find ways to create incremental business efficiencies and incremental improvements in our society and environment.

We can make an impact by making sure a company's distribution logistics are environmentally friendly. We can make an impact by reducing profit making by eliminating harmful tactics, such as employing cheaper production methods. We can make an impact by researching and deploying new technologies that are less harmful to the environment or through new environmental regulations to legislate a better society.

While all of the above opportunities will yield results, we can do even better when we focus on business model innovation. Business models, like SunEdison's, are revolutionary: they deliver compelling profits plus improve the environment. They mutually reinforce each other:

more profits results in more environmental improvement. These models provide more than just incremental improvements; they create breakthroughs and unlock opportunities.

Think of what Jigar Shah has done with SunEdison. He got the world's biggest retailers to put solar panels on their rooftops and replace some of their dirty coal-generated electricity with fossil-free solar.

It was not that companies like Wal-Mart weren't willing to use solar energy; they were just not interested in allocating funds in their fixed capital budgets to solar panels. The payback was too slow and the expenditure was not core to their main business. The requirement to make a steep upfront capital expenditure for many years of electricity savings was pain point that was holding Wal-Mart and other companies back from using solar energy. In fact, that kept the entire solar industry from growing.

SunEdison addressed this not by a technology innovation but by a business model innovation that eliminated the biggest customer pain point. Their business model innovation allowed them to offer customers like Wal-Mart to pay only for the energy they consumed, just like they would with any other utility. With this new business model in place, SunEdison unlocked potential that was there all along and they grew more rapidly than any other solar energy company before to become the largest provider of solar energy in the United States. Read the book to find out how exactly Jigar Shah and SunEdison pulled this off.

What is particularly exciting is that Jigar Shah is not alone. There is a whole new breed of entrepreneurs and so-called intrapreneurs who want to have an impact beyond profit. I see an increasing number of people like Jigar Shah across the globe in the companies and leading universities that I visit, like Stanford, IMD, Wharton, IESE, and Skolkovo. They are entering into large corporations or launching companies of their own right now.

The Principles

The key to unlocking opportunities for impact is a set of principles that characterize business model innovations that go beyond profit.

*Profit and impact can go hand in hand and even reinforce
each other.*

While an increasing number of entrepreneurs, senior executives, bankers, venture capitalists, and academics understand this, it was not common wisdom. Traditionally, we separated impact and profit-seeking activities. Nonprofit organizations and corporate social responsibility teams in large companies focused on impact, while corporate executives and entrepreneurs focused on making money. This wall between focusing on profit or focusing on impact is breaking down. Jigar Shah's SunEdison is just one example of a company producing spectacular success in terms of financial returns and environmental impact through new business models.

However, this development is not limited to environmental impact; the same is happening in the social sector and economic development. Grameen Phone, for example, which was founded by Iqbal Quadir, gave rural Bangladesh access to mobile telecommunications by getting women in villages to sell phone services based on a microcredit system. This business model innovation turned Grameen Phone into the biggest taxpayer in that country and improved the wealth and social status of tens of thousands of women throughout rural Bangladesh. A great emerging example is Peepoople, a for-profit and venture-funded startup that aims to solve one of the biggest issues in the world: the fact that 2.6 billion people lack access to proper sanitation. Peepoople is deliberately for-profit because they believe it's more sustainable than the nonprofit approach.

What characterizes all the above examples is the fact that the more profit they make, the more impact is achieved. One does not come at the expense of the other. Of course, we can't address every single one of the world's problems with for-profit models, yet, as Michael Shuman, author of *Going Local*, nicely summarizes, the nonprofits' approach should be complemented by new approaches: "There's a very good argument that many of the attributes of typical nonprofits—heavy reporting requirements, self-reappointing boards, poor access to capital, awful labor standards (in the name of the public interest)—make them lousy vehicles for social change…I think we need to rethink the structure of do-good enterprises." I have seen this firsthand when I helped build a global nonprofit organization in the health sector before becoming an entrepreneur myself.

Breakthrough growth can be achieved without technology or product innovation.

Another long-held belief is that technology innovation is our best bet to solve some of the biggest issues of our time. This is simply not true. SunEdison, Grameen Phone, and Peepoople are all examples that demonstrate that breakthroughs can be achieved without technology innovation. Sometimes breakthroughs can even be achieved with inferior technologies.

Of course this requires a change in mindset. Most companies—startups and Fortune 500 companies alike—still spend most of their research-and-development budgets on technology and product innovation. Yet we need to change our focus if we accept that better business models can lead to success, just like technology and product innovation did on their own in the past. Rather than pouring all our resources into technology and product innovation, we need to mobilize time and resources for the search for the right business model. Technology and product innovation are not bad, of course, but even the greatest technologies and products will fail to succeed without a viable business model.

One of the moments that left the biggest mark on me in my career was when the head of R&D of a large company told me that they were going to dig into their database of failed projects to figure out if any of those could succeed with a better business model. The lesson here is that there is a lot of potential to be unearthed within existing resources if we just take the time to search for the right business models.

Fail cheaply, fail quickly, and fail often to succeed sooner.

Innovation and entrepreneurship never happen without experimentation, and experimentation rarely, if ever, happens without failure. What characterizes successful innovators is their ability to continuously test their assumptions about the world and adapt accordingly. Failing and being wrong is a positive thing as long as it is quick, cheap, and leads to learning and evolution. Successful innovators and entrepreneurs use this process of rapid evolution to turn their assumptions into facts and build.

The search for scalable business models that make a profit and have an impact is no easy undertaking. Solutions will not fall from the sky. You will have to test your assumptions about what customers are trying to get done, what they are struggling with, and what they are trying to achieve. You will have to test your assumptions about what creates value for them, how they want to be reached, and what they are willing to pay for. As my friend Steve Blank, a Silicon Valley entrepreneur turned educator, likes to say: "No business plan survives the first contact with customers." You will have to pivot your business model and elements of it countless times until you find a profitable and scalable business model that has an impact.

Ideas are cheap.

Mass media often limit their stories of successful entrepreneurs and executives to the shiny side. They often sketch out a picture of the creative and persistent genius that just happened to have the right idea. While this is part of the story, media mostly fails to mention the trail of sweat, failure, and hardship that usually precedes success. Don't get misled by this. Ideas are cheap.

The Tools and Processes of the Entrepreneurial Game

Over the last decade, I have researched and built tools that help build better business models. I started with a PhD and ended up as a software entrepreneur cofounding Strategyzer.com. While I'm proud my work is being applied in large companies and startups alike, I am most excited that my work is helping people like Jigar Shah who are striving for impact.

Jigar Shah's story is amazing, and it took him a lot of sweat equity to get there. Achieving what he has will always be hard, but I was amazed to discover that many of the tools and processes that are currently revolutionizing entrepreneurship can help do more systematically what Jigar Shah has accomplished by gut feeling and perseverance. One of them, as mentioned, is the Business Model Canvas, a tool that helps you systematically describe and design better business models. The other is Customer Development and Lean Startup, two processes that help you periodically test business models by turning assumptions into facts. Try them out in combination with the fantastic advice, lessons, and facts outlined in this book. I thoroughly enjoyed every page of it. And, through this book, I hope you discover your Business Model Beyond Profit.

Alexander Osterwalder, Echandens, Switzerland, April 2013

Introduction

Creating Climate Wealth: Unlocking the Impact Economy

Never doubt that a small group of thoughtful committed citizens can change the world; indeed, it's the only thing that ever has.
—Margaret Mead

The reason for this book is to make the case that the solar industry has become a $100-billion industry because it was designed and structured by entrepreneurs that used mainstream investors not impact investors. This truth, about the role of impact investors in unlocking climate change solutions, could prevent approximately $10 trillion of mainstream capital from streaming into these solutions. There is a false choice often being made between high impact and high returns. We can have both. In fact, we must achieve both to achieve scale and unlock the greatest wealth creation opportunity of our time.

This opportunity begins with people. I am lucky. I have been one small voice in the world that was one of the first to attract mainstream capital to solar. I used a new business model to deploy solar energy that unlocked a multibillion-dollar solar energy services industry. Through hard work, timing, good luck, and demand, it has spawned hundreds of thousands of jobs and has made many people wealthy; it produces clean electricity close to customers—and continues to grow today at exponential rates.

Even though people may think this is an incredible story, the point is that it is really an attainable story and one that we can repeat again and again—not only to build more than one multibillion-dollar industry but rather to build many multibillion-dollar industries. If the International Energy Agency is right, it will add up to a new $10-trillion economy—while solving our global climate and environmental issues. This is what I mean by "creating climate wealth."

Today, after the fact, investments in solar energy have been classified as impact investing, not socially responsible investing. The reality is that solar energy was really started by mainstream investors looking for financially compelling returns in an industry that happened to be "green." Recently, impact investments have captured people's imaginations. Impact investors concern themselves with finding investment opportunities that deliver both a financially compelling return and a positive impact on the environment or society. Yet most of these investors limit their impact investments to a small part of their portfolio because they believe they must sacrifice financial return to achieve the highest societal impact. I wholeheartedly disagree.

Impact investments can drive incredible wealth opportunities—and create a new economy. It is what I call, and the Carbon War Room has deemed, climate wealth creation.

To optimize climate wealth creation, we need structure. Structure assumes discipline. It helps investors choose between projects that have passed muster as opposed to projects with buzz that fizzle because they have no sustainable growth potential. It sets guidance parameters so investors find investments that will create new industries that deliver perpetual financial growth and return.

With rising commodity costs, water shortages, and global warming, the world market potential for these investments is enormous. A key reason is that many technologies exist that have already been tested and proven. We simply need to deploy them in a way that makes business sense. It is a precise focus on the deployment of existing technologies that will drive economic growth and jobs and create climate wealth—our next economy. For those who argue for innovation first, I would say that in this sector, only technology deployment and wealth creation from that deployment drives sustained interest in innovation funding; choosing one over the other is a false choice.

If the path to creating climate wealth will create a new economy, our impact investments need to go beyond being emotionally compelling investments. They need structure and business-model discipline to prove to traditional investors that the opportunities are solid. I will examine this idea throughout this book.

In just the last five years, about $1 trillion has been invested in the deployment of renewable electricity—most of it from mainstream capital sources. In 2013, the Global Impact Investing Network estimates that $9 billion will be committed to impact investments, a 12.5-percent increase from the $8 billion committed in 2012. Unfortunately, most of that money will never attract mainstream capital. As followers; we must change that.

The time has arrived when we must invest this money into opportunities that offer compelling financial returns and demonstrate the scale needed to impact climate change. We need investments that are part of the building blocks of driving a new industry. In fact, we can't afford to waste our time or money on investments that do not drive a new industry. This is not about a short-term buck but rather a long-term fix.

So we must identify and invest in the businesses that can unlock the $10 trillion necessary to solve climate change. This is a big number; this book will show you how we can get there. The key is making sure we have the discipline to never compromise financial returns for societal returns—at least not in the impact investment space.

This book is about how a small group of people *can* lead a revolution from the "feel-good," socially responsible investment that is attracting $9 billion in 2013 to impact investments that build solid businesses in perpetuity—ones that become the lion's share of investor portfolios. Why? Simple: the financial returns are compelling, and the social and environmental impact are awe-inspiring.

As noted, I know this from personal experience. Much of my story and the story of the company I founded, SunEdison, are in this book. This is not a biography or history; rather, it is a testament to what can be done and an attempt to make clear the path to change. The opportunities are real. We have more to do in solar and much more to do in industries like shipping, building efficiency, industrial efficiency, heavy trucks, agriculture, and others we discuss later in the book.

The solutions, the technology, and the demand exist. What is needed is a well-oiled machine devoid of the persistent friction that clogs the capital flow to impact investments. We can't wait for the Wall Street establishment; they lost the willpower to solve real problems long ago. We need a bastion of motivated entrepreneurs and investors to step up and execute. There is good to be done and a huge amount of wealth to be created if it is done correctly.

Our new wave of smart impact investing yields consistent returns—ones that make professional investors consider them on equal footing with other parts of their profit-generating portfolio. In order to meet basic fundamental investment criteria, each must simultaneously achieve the following goals:

- Solve pressing problems for consumers
- Yield impressive risk-adjusted returns for investors
- Generate both development and economic growth; politicians do not want to choose!
- Create local capacity that is independently sustainable and does not require the continual interjection of outside foreign firms to fix problems

We have at our disposal right now the power, knowledge, know-how, technology, resources, and proven solutions to change and improve our world. There are achievable strategies in this book with returns and benefits that are substantial—and sustainable. They create climate wealth.

After selling SunEdison, I started investing my own capital in impact investments. I have attracted investors into solar photovoltaic, solar thermal, hydroponics, gasified biomass, and other areas. Why? Each investment delivers compelling financial returns, creates jobs, and solves a pressing local problem today—and tomorrow.

In the pages ahead, I will share more of my story, including some of the lessons other motivated entrepreneurs and I have learned, and I will point to the real opportunities that exist to make these lessons tangible and real.

I do understand it is hard to comprehend things on a trillion-dollar scale because few can conceptualize that kind of money. All of us have trouble imagining solutions of that magnitude. Believe me, though, they are out there. The opportunities are exciting, and the timing is right. We need to begin to really have an impact and seize what lies before us. It will benefit the people and the planet, and it will drive enormous profit: impactful profit and the creation of climate wealth.

It does start with one person and then another—then another. Take it from me: just one small voice that joined with other small voices to engage a small group of committed citizens who, in turn, created (and changed) a $100-billion industry.

One more thought...

Before you read this book, please note that it is not about perfection; it is about deployment.

While many philosophize about the perfect solution or technology for clean energy solutions and climate change, this book focuses on the *practical deployment of the best* technologies that exist—technologies we have been piloting for over 15 years. The views expressed in this book are solely my own and are not intended to be the views of SunEdison, The Carbon War Room, or any other person or entity.

So, for example, while manufacturing solar panels may create carbon emissions, the energy returned on energy invested from solar far exceeds the same measurement from unconventional oil. The bottom line is that it is worth it.

If we waited for the perfect technology, we would not have a chance to solve the business model and finance model challenges. Simply put, we would run out of time.

And, we have seen that when we wait for perfection, it works against us. A case in point is waste to energy. While using waste as a fuel source can create energy, it also creates toxins in the environment. So, we make no real decision on waste to energy while garbage that could be recycled and repurposed overflows in landfills, creating a more everlasting environmental problem.

So while time is not on our side, this book is optimistic about the value in deploying now to accelerate progress. Transformational improvements in the sectors that are ready for it beats sitting idle.

And as we make progress day by day, Voltaire would say, "Très bien" ("Very good").

Section I:
Hypothesis, My Story, and How the World Works

CHAPTER ONE:
My Hypothesis

*"I'd put my money on the sun and solar power…I hope we don't
have to wait until oil and gas run out until we tackle that."*
—Thomas Edison

By the time I graduated from high school, I was convinced that the
whole world would one day be powered by solar and nuclear energy.
I'm not sure why I felt so strongly about it. It was intuition or gut
instinct— a feeling I couldn't have justified at the time.

That unshakable belief can be traced back to when I was sixteen, growing up in Sterling, Illinois, a small, whistle-stop, rural town where my
father practiced medicine. He was a general practitioner, a rapidly forgotten medical practice on the American landscape.

My dad gave me a short, twenty-page picture book about energy that
he bought from a college student selling the books door to door. I was
not interested at the time and so the book must have gathered dust for
a few years on a shelf in the living room until I was sixteen. I have no
idea what prompted me to pull the book off the shelf and rapidly leaf
through it. But I'll always remember how its contents fired my imagination, igniting a passion that has never been extinguished to this day. That
book changed my life and became the foundation for my career.

Initially, the pictures captured my attention more than the flimsy text.
Each of the book's six chapters—each one had two facing pages—were

about the principal energy sources: coal, natural gas, nuclear, hydro, wind, and solar.

After reading the short book several times, I kept on returning to the sections on nuclear and solar particularly. I didn't know anything about energy, but I thought solar was pretty damn cool. I thought that sparsely populated areas such as Sterling should be solar powered cities, because they were so dense, ought to be powered by nuclear energy.

I assumed that because each chapter in the book had two pages, all energies were equal. I didn't know that coal, natural gas, and nuclear dominated our world, and wind and solar were irrelevant back then.

From that moment on, I was determined to learn everything I could about solar power. I was also interested in nuclear energy, but it was my hypothesis that solar would someday power the world that I wanted to prove—until someone debunked it. No one could.

My teachers knew little more than I did about solar energy. My search began. Keep in mind there was no way to Google information then. The Internet was not widely available. I was fueled instead by imagination and an occasional *Popular Science* article.

Everyone I talked with said he or she had a positive gut feeling about solar and nuclear energy. The general consensus was that these power sources had enormous possibilities and were destined for big things.

I remember my high school math teacher cornering me and saying, "You are right, Jigar, solar is pretty interesting. Good boy. Keep working on it."

I don't think she cared all that much about it, but she was polite enough not to discourage me and kill my dream.

Nine years later, in 1999, my early hypothesis about solar was confirmed when I landed my first serious solar job with BP Solar. But my feelings about nuclear's economic realities had changed. The cost of harnessing nuclear power on a large scale in every country except China was actually increasing. And nuclear power stations' cooling towers require more water than most coal plants do. The only alternative to the water usage associated with nuclear energy is more expensive dry cooling. And nuclear-waste issues have yet to be resolved.

I never shelved my belief in the power and impact of nuclear power. I am still pro-nuclear but just cannot see how large multibillion-dollar projects make financial sense. It could make sense for smaller projects. Small modular reactors, or SMRs, are being used throughout the world, pioneered by the US military, because they're a cost-efficient and flexible way to power ships at sea. The terrestrial version would be mass-manufactured and brought to a site ready to install, saving an enormous amount of time, labor, and cost by avoiding on-site construction.

Belief in Solar Reinforced

Meanwhile, the more I learned, the more my belief in solar was repeatedly reinforced. Even cynics and skeptics admitted that although they didn't understand solar power, they said it would be nice to figure out—a conclusion at which I had already arrived. But the confirmation, if nothing else, was inspiring.

Searching for a college in which to study solar energy wasn't easy. It was hardly a popular major. Many people suggested that I get an engineering degree. Looking back, it made sense. Engineering was really valuable even if it wasn't my first passion.

I decided to attend the University of Illinois, Urbana-Champaign, at the suggestion of one of its researchers, Ty A. Newell, who had written extensively about solar ponds. Even though I didn't have the personality of an engineer and knew even then that I wanted to be an entrepreneur, he persuaded me to study mechanical engineering, allowing me to design my own major because there were so many electives. That translated into a perfect opportunity to study solar and gather information to support my hypothesis.

Fueling My Entrepreneurial Passion

Even as a kid, I knew I wanted to be an entrepreneur. I can thank my family for teaching me entrepreneurial basics—the importance of being self-reliant and thinking for myself. These principles were ingrained in me as far back as I could remember. I grew up in a family of overachievers, doers in the best sense of the word. They taught me that there are certain things we can change and other things that are out of our control. I still remember every word of Reinhold Niebuhr's *Serenity Prayer*, which was framed on my mother 's night table:

> *God, grant me the serenity to accept the things I cannot change,*
> *courage to change the things I can,*
> *and wisdom to know the difference.*

More than an eloquent and beautifully written poem, it was a philosophy of life for my family. To this day, its prophetic verse still guides me. It's also one of the indestructible bulwarks for being a successful entrepreneur. It motivated me to excel, to be as good as I can possibly be. I've never been a complainer. If something is wrong, I try to fix it rather than throw in the towel and move on. With that steadfast, focused mindset, I embraced solar with an unstoppable passion, fueled by boundless energy.

I worked a string of part-time jobs because I thought being self-sufficient would be a good thing. I chose a job that would let me find time to study solar. One job in particular—working nights in a dormitory—stands out because it gave me the opportunity to take advantage of the university's computer lab, which boasted cutting-edge technology for its day. It housed the country's first popular graphical Internet browser, Mosaic, which was developed by a team including Marc Andreessen, who went on to co-found Netscape.

At the time, the Internet was commercialized at the university level. With an empty computer lab to myself, I couldn't have asked for a more idyllic research environment. The North Carolina Solar Center had hundreds of files on a file transfer protocol (FTP) site. I downloaded every file I could find on solar, about one hundred, mostly about passive solar. I printed them on a dot-matrix printer and stored them in two fat binders, each with five hundred pages.

Because solar energy wasn't taught at universities, I was among a handful of people around the world who was seriously researching it. In the early to mid-1990s, solar was a hobby, and the people who studied it shared their files on FTP servers.

By the time I graduated, I was more convinced than ever that my hypothesis was bulletproof. There was no question in my mind that it was only a matter of time before the world would be powered by solar. I was hell-bent on getting a job in the industry.

Not that the other energy sources weren't valid. Wind power, for one, never excited me because it was large-scale, not necessarily local. Also, sometimes the wind blows; sometimes it doesn't. But the sun is every-where. It's unfailingly—even mystically—predictable. I understood why it was the basis for the Hindu Gayatri mantra:

> *Oh God, Thou art the Giver of Life, Remover of pain and sorrow,*
> *The Bestower of happiness, Oh! Creator of the Universe,*
> *May we receive thy supreme sin-destroying light, May Thou guide*
> *our intellect in the right direction.*

I learned a great deal about solar at the University of Illinois, but it didn't mean that much because solar jobs were hard to find. I wasn't greeted with a beckoning job market desperate to test my knowledge, enthusiasm, and passion. I scoured the country to find companies that were even remotely connected to this nascent industry. The few com-panies out there were hardly more than startup operations struggling to survive.

I finally landed a job at a startup company in Vermont that made wind turbines. I drove cross-country in my Toyota pickup to take a job paying $30,000 a year.

It turned out to be a classic, if not clichéd, entrepreneurial experience. The company was already teetering on the brink of bankruptcy when I arrived. As for my salary, I saw only $6,000 of the promised $30,000.

I wasn't cheated or duped. The company's founder had every intention of paying me, and the rest of his staff as well. But promised funding never materialized. Prospective customers backed out at the last min-ute. When my boss couldn't meet his payroll, the full-time staff stopped coming to work. And for good reason. They had wives, children, and mortgages. If I had been in their place, I would have done the same thing, but I was twenty-two, and I had only myself to support.

Life has a strange and wonderful way of working itself out. At the time, the ideals of the *Serenity Prayer* came back to me: living one day at a time, enjoying one moment at a time, and accepting hardships as the pathway to peace.

In *When It Hits the Fan*, Gerald C. Meyers (former chair of American Motors) said that heroes are often born in a crisis.

I certainly didn't see myself as a hero, but I sensed that hardship often creates opportunities. And this was a learning experience not to be passed up.

I took a part-time job at a nearby grocery store to cover my living expenses and kept coming to work every day. It was just my boss and me.

I quickly learned to be a jack-of-all-trades and master of none of them. I was a janitor, business-plan writer, and accountant. When I left a year later, I had learned a lot about startup companies, especially what happens when there isn't any money coming in. What I did see at the wind company definitely informed my thoughts for the later idea that became SunEdison. In case after case, when we worked on the deals with prospective clients who were mostly farmers, they balked when they came to understand what the upfront cost would be. They were interested in having the energy but did not want to part with the $80,000 to $100,000 the installation would cost. Return on investment (ROI) did not matter. And they really did not want to be in the energy business. A different model was needed that would cover the cost of the equipment over time.

I moved to Washington, DC, to take a job with a consulting company whose only client was the US Department of Energy. Actually, I was a Beltway bandit, a slang term for a temp worker who did whatever he or she was told. I took on a variety of projects, such as writing reports and studies about alternative energies and putting together PowerPoint presentations. It was also a valuable experience because I learned what makes our capital tick, how the power politics game is played, and, most importantly, how not to get things done.

During this period, I enrolled at the University of Maryland in College Park to get my MBA. I had figured out that I did not want to be an engineer, and most of what is really involved in business was foreign to me due to the highly technical nature of the engineering program. If I was going to be marketable in the business community, I needed a business background. I did not approach the MBA with SunEdison in mind; the business plan was born in a course. It was yet another valuable opportunity to flesh out my hypothesis about solar energy and write the business plan for SunEdison, which was an assignment for an entrepreneurship class I took. I got an A for the business plan, further confirmation that all my assertions about solar were on the money.

But I temporarily shelved the idea of launching SunEdison to take a job with BP Solar as a business analyst in its mergers-and-acquisitions department—a smart move that turned out to be a hugely valuable experience. Having written the business plan for SunEdison, I found BP a great place to test my ideas. It was an amazing experience because many smart people mentored me. It was also an indescribable ego-booster for me as such a young person. I realized the impact and value of working for the world's third-largest energy company. Suddenly, people treated me differently. Prior to joining BP, no one wanted to talk to me when I called to pitch an idea. That changed when I joined BP. As soon as I said I worked there, I had people's undivided attention.

Not only did my stint with BP do wonders for my confidence, but it also taught me the value of brand and the clout of a high-powered business card. BP also encouraged me to pitch my business plan for SunEdison. BP turned it down but said it had merit. I didn't give up on the idea; I just put it on hold until I could get more traction behind it. One of my professors, who was a venture capitalist, said, "Jigar, you've got a great business plan, but right now," which was the height of the dot-com boom, "nobody wants to mess with infrastructure."

So I put it on hold until the timing was right, which was September 2003, when I left BP to launch SunEdison. The rest, as they say, is history.

CHAPTER TWO:

Our Natural Systems are Failing Us

"We don't have an energy problem; we have an oil addiction problem."
—The nonpartisan Fuel Freedom.org

In this chapter, I am going to diverge a bit from my story, to provide an overview of the issues we face in energy and infrastructure – with a focus on the U.S. It will serve as a backdrop when I outline some of the opportunities before us to create the $10 trillion economy. I will also reference some leading voices in the field on their perspective regarding the crisis and the role we, and governments, should play, and will discuss where the money will come from to drive $10 trillion in investment.

First, most people engaged in solving the problems of climate change have been motivated by saving the planet – an entrepreneurial opportunity – or both.

While I generally stay closer to the entrepreneurship side vs. the environmentalist side, working in the renewable energy space really does require the context of both. For me, the motivating environmental story starts with the oil crises. The 1973 and 1979 oil crises pointed to a serious problem that impacted the global economy and energized an entire generation of scientists and inventors.

Governments, including the United States, admitted that they were vulnerable to OPEC and energy price volatility. The immediate response was an unprecedented investment in research to diversify our energy mix and create alternative technologies to hedge against future actions to raise the price of oil.

Fast-forward thirty years. George W. Bush, then President of the United States, said, "America is addicted to oil, which is often imported from unstable parts of the world. The best way to break this addiction is through technology."

Bush wasn't the first American President to say he wanted to wean his nation from a Middle Eastern oil addiction. In 1971, President Richard M. Nixon promised to make the United States energy self-sufficient by 1980. Eight years later, in 1979, President Jimmy Carter said the United States "would never again use more foreign oil than we did in 1977."

The nonpartisan Fuel Freedom.org (www.fuelfreedom.org) recently wrote, "We don't have an energy problem, we have an oil addiction problem." University of California's (San Diego) economist James Hamilton, who correlated US economic activity with oil prices, said that ten of the last eleven recessions were preceded by spikes in oil prices. In 2008, energy expert Amory Lovins, author of *Winning the Oil Endgame*, said the world's "biggest untapped energy source is efficiency. And retooling for energy efficiency will require 'barrier-busting' at many levels." As for government's role, Lovins added it "should steer, not row."

Retired US Navy Lieutenant Robert Diamond is one of many people who have summed it up this way: Some people take pictures of their food. I think you have a good niche for yourself! "America's reliance on oil is our Achilles heel." He went on to say that "at the very core of my war-time deployment was an energy-security mission." In 2006, after giving his testimony to a Senate subcommittee, Milton Copulus, head of the National Defense Council Foundation, said that Senators Lugar and Biden were, in his words, "stunned" by how much the United States was spending to defend the oil of the Persian Gulf. "Senator Lugar actually had been aware of our earlier figure of $49.1 billion, but this $132.7 billion annual figure—that's every year—really kind of shook him up" (Moore, 2006).

Meanwhile, the National Academy of Science said that $120 billion per year is spent mostly by the US government to allay the health-related side effects caused by using burning fossil fuels like coal for electricity and oil for vehicles (Wald, 2009). Further, the energy sector, not agriculture, accounts for 49 percent of all water used in the United States. Add new efforts around hydraulic fracturing to the mix, and the 49 percent is probably higher today.

Why can't the US—which has spearheaded innovation on countless fronts, ranging from pioneering the Apollo Space Mission, Silicon Valley, the mobile phone revolution, and the electrical grid—kick this habit? For that matter, why can't it deploy technology that pays for itself in sectors like electricity, water, and waste?

Why is the United States—once a trendsetting global industrial leader—stuck in a complex quagmire of inefficiencies, out-of-control spending, and massive debt? Nobel Prize-winning economist Paul Krugman was recently quoted saying, "The U.S. economy is recovering but slowly" and is still experiencing "depression conditions. Almost four million workers have been out of work for more than a year…we haven't had anything like that since the '30s [and]… there's lots of unused capacity…a lot of savings that have nowhere to go (Napach, 2013). Well said. We have had "savings that have nowhere to go" in the energy sector for a very long time.

Our inability to deploy the technology we invented to solve these major problems is leading to a substantial economic loss.

In 2003, the Northeast experienced a devastating power outage—the second most widespread blackout in history—affecting more than 55 million people in the United States and Ontario and costing more than $6 billion in economic output (Minkel, 2008). More recently, New York, New Jersey, and Connecticut had a multiday power outage because of Hurricane Sandy. It is estimated that the US loses power for at least four hours per year due to natural disasters; in Germany, by way of comparison, it was 15.3 minutes in 2011, counting all natural disasters.

Making matters worse, the United States. is not just behind on the electricity grid, but it is $2 trillion behind in infrastructure improvements (roads, water, sewer, flood control, essential public improvements).

How Did We Get Here?

Putting aside the consequences, how did we get into the situation where private industry was able to dump real costs onto the public in a non-transparent way?

Some of our citizens have an adverse reaction to coal and oil burning, the consequences of which are paid for by public and private healthcare providers through the impact on peoples' health, and the energy sector doesn't even pay one-tenth of what we pay at home for the fresh water they use, giving them little incentive to recycle or reuse the water.

It is frustrating that we have invented and tested, at scale, all of the technologies necessary to slash our fuel consumption by 50 percent, make buildings 50 percent more energy efficient, help agriculture free itself from the burden of high oil prices, divert 50 percent of our garbage and waste into productive income-earning opportunities, and find and repair leaks in our water system, which results in a 40-percent loss rate after chemically treating our municipal fresh water.

Given the state of our infrastructure, deploying solutions we have already invented represents the largest wealth-creation opportunity of our lifetime and does not require government money, just government leadership.

Factor in investments that could be made in the US and the exports that could be made deploying American technology around the world. This next wave represents a $10-trillion opportunity. And this is not a hypothetical estimate but a realistic one—if not underestimated—quantified by the International Energy Agency, Accenture, Booz-Allen, HSBC, Bloomberg New Energy Finance, and other respected organizations.

What's Holding Us Back?

Creating and managing infrastructure has been the domain of the federal government. But most governments have forgotten how to do it. In the US, electricity and water infrastructure was largely built before 1980. Today, the responsibility for both electricity infrastructure and water infrastructure is now the province of local and state governments—most of which no longer have the expertise to do anything radically different than in their grandfathers' generation, not to mention the lack of funding available at either level in most cases.

Transportation, which has a big federal government component, is one of the least innovative industries on the planet. What is thwarting innovation is the huge barrier to entry. Consider Tesla, the new electric car company. Tesla made it because it had a deep-pocketed backer in PayPal founder, Elon Musk. Designing a car is a long and expensive process, but if you have the money to do that you still need to spend enormous sums of money to actually get it approved to sell. This involves interacting with federal government agencies that only have one way of doing things, expensively.

Unless an entrepreneur launches a successful Internet start-up first (PayPal, for example), it's almost impossible to raise sufficient capital to succeed in this space. In fact, all forms of transportation, rail, new roads, or new engines that offer fuel choice require rigorous government testing and approval procedures. To start a new company in transportation simply takes billions.

Amory Lovins invented the HyperCar and inspired Bright Automotive, but neither of them was able to significantly impact the auto business despite their amazing technology and lofty goals. One of the reasons he was unsuccessful was because he couldn't raise the capital to hire lobbyists and regulatory specialists needed to build a street-legal car. So he changed the business model to license his technology to the big automakers. Compare this to the solar electricity industry, where entrepreneurs can complete the requirements to receive their safety stickers from Underwriters Laboratory for less than $150,000.

That's only half the problem. The other half is that this is the decade of government austerity. Even if the government wanted to step in and make the process more accessible, they couldn't. Each federal agency would have to build more test facilities and hire hundreds of additional staff to handle the additional workload. Trying to convince Congress to spend taxpayer money on such a herculean task is difficult at best.

Yet there is a clear, realizable, and attainable solution within our grasp that can fix much of our decaying infrastructure and save our crippled and impotent economy so it can reclaim its once-dominant position as a global industry leader.

Small is Beautiful – Power by The Hour

The answer lies in adopting two paradigms that have gone underre-
ported. The first is that while "bigger is better" was the guiding paradigm
for industrial growth in the twentieth century, what will take the United
States into a new and better future in the twenty-first century is "small
is beautiful," made popular by British economist E.F. Schumacher, who
wrote *Small Is Beautiful: Economics As If People Mattered* in 1973. To
stress the importance of Schumacher's cutting-edge observations and,
most importantly, that he had his hand on the pulse of the future, his
book received the prestigious Prix Européen de l'Essai Charles Veillon in
1976, and *The Times Literary Supplement* ranked his book among the
most influential published since World War II.

The new paradigm applies to innumerable projects: power plants,
transportation, water purification, agriculture, and energy efficiency.
It's easier and more efficient to deploy 1,000 $1-million projects than
deploying a single $1-billion project. Here are the reasons:

> ➤ Small projects are easier to get off the ground. They're not
>   bogged down by bureaucratic red tape and endless approval
>   layers.
> ➤ Small projects don't require a multi-stakeholder process. Most
>   can be installed for one owner on private property.
> ➤ In the wake of a banking shakeout and crisis, banks prefer
>   financing small (but not tiny) projects. Most large banks can't
>   provide capital on their own for projects exceeding $100 million
>   anymore.
> ➤ It's also difficult finding working capital to fund construction
>   and key business functions for large projects, especially for new
>   technologies.
> ➤ Lastly, most of these projects need a local political backer with
>   strong connections to push them through all of the regulatory
>   hurdles—or lead to outright corruption. Finding stakeholders for
>   a $1-million project rarely has the same problems in this area as
>   with a $1-billion project.

The second guiding paradigm for the twenty-first century is infrastructure as a service. As Rolls Royce calls it, "Power by the hour." The
best infrastructure solutions generally cost more upfront and have low

operating costs. As with majestic bridges and well-planned cities, quality costs more upfront. This is also true for renewable electricity solutions like solar and hydropower or vehicle solutions like electric and natural gas vehicles. Buyers have to pay more upfront and save on operating costs over time.

The way Rolls Royce does it is that instead of selling a very expensive aircraft engine, they simply charge the airline a fixed fee for every hour the engine runs. That price covers all the costs including maintenance while having enough profit built in to pay shareholders back in full. The customer loves this concept because they save the upfront investment and all of the maintenance staff required to maintain an aircraft engine. With an asset life of over ten to twenty years, customers can get access to the best infrastructure that saves them money over the longer term.

In Pacific Gas and Electric Company's territory, for example, there is more than $1 billion in solar projects planned every year. There is no financial mechanism for PG&E (or other regulated government utilities) to raise $1 billion from Wall Street to fund these solar projects through their unregulated subsidiaries to compete. But individual solar projects on the rooftops of quality customers have attracted money from Google, Morgan Stanley, Wells Fargo, MetLife, MassMutual, Warren Buffett, and others to deploy the necessary $15 billion for United States solar projects in 2012.

There is a pattern here most people don't know about. There are rules and strategies to this new approach to infrastructure. I have successfully deployed them, and so have others. The reason I am sharing them with you is that we need help. There are simply not enough of us. Without help, we won't achieve scale.

Whether you want clean electricity, water, agriculture, buildings, industry, vehicles, or other solutions, to make a difference in climate change, job creation, or economic growth in any of these sectors we have to invest at least $1 trillion by 2020.

That is only a beginning. Bloomberg New Energy Finance and the International Energy Agency predict that we will successfully shift over $3 trillion into these solutions by 2020, which is a fantastic start most people don't even know about. But to actually achieve real progress in tackling climate change and reducing all of the health impact from fossil fuel pollution outlined by the National Academy of Science, we must deploy more than just the $3 trillion globally for renewable electricity projects.

More than $3 trillion is necessary to 1) eliminate our dependence on oil through efficiency and substitution, 2) upgrade our outdated water infrastructure, 3) update our fossil fuel fertilizer supply chain, and 4) really meet the capital needs necessary to meet the climate-change goals of two degrees set by the leaders of the free world. The electricity sector alone needs $5 trillion, and the rest of the sectors will have to contribute about $5 trillion more.

Where will this money come from? For starters, there is more than $125 trillion available in investment funds: pension funds, insurance companies, sovereign wealth funds, and large family offices around the world. And they are investing heavily in US treasuries and other safe investments that pay very low interest rates. The pension funds and insurance companies need to earn about 8 percent annually to meet their obligations—and many of them are falling woefully short. The only way for them to meet this rate of return is to invest in what is called "infrastructure"—long-dated investments that usually return 8 to 11 percent after accounting for the fees charged by investment professionals. The 2013 World Economic Forum in Davos estimated that $5 trillion in new infrastructure was going to happen anyway each year. We simply have to shift about 20 to 30 percent of that spending away from fossil-fuel-related projects and toward equivalent climate-change solutions. Additionally, the only sector deep enough to absorb all this money in search of returns today is infrastructure—the sector that is the key to solving climate change.

What's Holding Things Up?

Mainstream capital organizations like pension funds and insurance companies are very conservative organizations that need a well-thought-out plan with specific investment goals and opportunities that meet their requirements. They can't invest in ideas because they don't invest in things that are not concrete—at least not at scale.

These investors require investment managers who understand what they are doing and choose to work in this space. These investment managers require portfolio managers who aggregate enough projects to be worth the time to study the situation and invest money into. The portfolio managers require developers who find prospective customers who meet the investors' strict criteria and approved technologies. The developers require inventors who not only have working solutions but ones that have been tested at scale with a manufacturing and installation team that delivers top-quality solutions over and over again.

It all takes a lot of coordination, which is why we haven't made much progress.

Sometimes the government forces coordination by providing rich incentives that cause developers and customers to clamor for solutions and everyone else to fall into line. This is what Jimmy Carter did for solar hot water, wind energy, and other technologies. And it is what the German government is doing now for renewable electricity. But it doesn't have to be done with money; the government can coordinate simply by convening and setting standards.

The developing world has to work that way because the need for infrastructure far outweighs the money available through agencies like the Overseas Private Investment Corporation, US Export Import Bank, United States Agency for International Development, the World Bank, and other institutions funded completely or partially by a donor community. All of these institutions are committed to solving problems such as providing access to modern energy and clean drinking water, but they have no plan and are not in charge of progress, just transactions. As a result, most of these organizations have made no perceptible difference on energy access and access to clean drinking water over the last 40 years.

And when there has been progress, such as Ashok Gadgil's UV Waterworks (http://mit.edu/invent/iow/gadgil.html), the numbers are measured in millions of people, not hundreds of millions. We either lose focus or expect that the market knows how to scale profitable solutions once a breakthrough has been achieved. To initiate change at scale, we must learn to coordinate technology deployment at scale. Simply pushing money through central governments down to local communities, like we did in the last century, won't work.

UV Waterworks created a unit that can purify one hundred liters of water for just two cents of solar electricity. But since local communities pay much more for water today from water trucks, one has to wonder if UV Waterworks could attract more capital if they charged more. Local communities are willing to pay for clean energy, clean water, and other services. The ability to pay can be monetized directly using a service-based model for infrastructure.

Alternatives to diesel-powered electricity serving the developing world seems to be another opportunity ready for immediate deployment. About 650 gigawatts of diesel generators (and other high-priced liquid fuels) are used to produce 5 percent of the global electricity used. With delivered diesel prices so high, they generate power at three to nine times what we pay from a well-functioning electricity grid. We have the technology to supply reliable energy to these populations cost effectively without building a grid but only at a 50-percent discount. Many aid agencies seemed to think, *If we can't save them 75 to 80 percent, we might as well not help them at all.* Most aid agencies thought they had a responsibility to match Western electricity prices, not acknowledging that poor people around the world are not living without energy; they just pay three to nine times more for it today. Furthermore, any grant money that was given was never mandated to figure out a way to attract private-sector capital after the grants ran out. As we will discuss, there is a process for making the transition, and it is pretty straightforward, if not always easy.

There are thousands of people who have dedicated their lives to deploying solutions to big problems at scale. None of these folks set out to make money, but all of the successful ones figured out how to make money—it was the only way to raise the mainstream capital needed to make a difference.

Creating Climate Wealth will resonate with frustrated governments, bureaucratic institutions, eager entrepreneurs, and yearning corporations. Today, many acknowledge that climate change is worse than anticipated, and progress-deploying solutions are slower than hoped. Many want the government to lead, citing China—the country with the highest emissions in the world—as the model of choice. Government can lead but not with money. With problems escalating and scale out of reach, a change of approach is required.

Now that you have this backdrop, I am going to demystify the process of accessing mainstream capital and present incontestable proof: success stories that can be replicated repeatedly. And we can start now. The result will be a thriving new society where constructive change is not only achieved, but massive, age-old infrastructure problems are rectified, all of which are led, directed, and implemented by a new class of entrepreneurs.

Let's not forget that American immigrant entrepreneurs were the impetus for this country's early growth. They paved the way for the world's household-name companies—all of which were once small entrepreneurial ventures. America's small companies have not only been the engines fueling growth but consistent job-creators as well.

In order to solve the problems outlined and create exciting new opportunities for tomorrow's entrepreneurs, here's what's needed.

1) **Deal flow**. To invest $10 trillion, we have to identify more than $10 trillion worth of projects worth pursuing. White papers and academic studies are great as far as they go, but only real projects with real contracts will fly. Investors can only invest in documented projects.

2) **Regulations**. In some places, deploying certain technologies is illegal or discouraged. It is important for entrepreneurs risking their hard-earned capital that the market is actually open for business. In the State of Georgia, customers who wish to finance their solar PV system through a "no-money-down" solar scheme are breaking the rules because only the electricity utility can sell power. Ridiculous nuances like this stifle deployment.

3) **Standards**. Investors have no idea whether a project will work unless they have a way to evaluate it to determine its feasibility. Investors rarely have the expertise to evaluate a project, making it necessary to bring in an independent third party to vouch for the project so all requirements are met and stakeholders' goals achieved. However, for small projects, hiring an independent third party is expensive, making standards critical so costs can be cut dramatically.

4) **Contractors**. There is no shortage of qualified professionals to do the engineering, procurement, and construction work, but only a small number are bonded and trusted by investors to get the job

done right the first time and meet investors' rigid requirements. We need more.

5) **Contracts**. Investors expect top-tier law firms to put together financeable contracts that will pass the test of time with a minimum of heartache. Experienced law firms know what has to be included and what can be improved.

6) **Maintenance**. All projects require maintenance. When developers create a pipeline of projects, most are paid when projects are successfully completed. Investors want assurance that competent, committed, and experienced operators will monitor and maintain performance after the initial commissioning is complete; twenty-five years is a long time to ensure good performance. They also want to make sure there is enough money in the budget to keep these operators motivated by compensating them fairly for their attention to detail.

7) **Government**. Someone has to control the chaos and be in charge of the overall plan. How will all of this infrastructure be managed and coordinated? For example, in the Eisenhower years, there was a master plan to build the infrastructure of our highway system. We need a master plan to build this new infrastructure, even as it's deployed on a small scale. How do new energy solutions fit with existing infrastructure? At what point is antiquated infrastructure retired? Does it all fit together, and how will we cope with new and unforeseen problems? How will massive change impact vital parts of the country's institutions?

I've outlined a few of the mounting problems facing the United States. Each year, they worsen, seriously impacting the global economy. The good news is that all of these problems can be solved. I am not offering hypothetical, theoretical solutions but ones that are practical and achievable. The chapters ahead will provide more proof around my assertions.

Why am I addressing these issues, and why should you listen to me? Who is Jigar Shah, and what makes me an energy authority? You're going to find out.

CHAPTER THREE:

My Story and SunEdison

In 2003, I kick-started SunEdison with $113,000—a $93,000 line of credit on my home and $20,000 in personal savings. For nine months, corporate headquarters was the first floor of my Washington, DC, townhome, where a couple of us worked without furniture around one phone. Then it was twelve months in a cramped, noisy, one-room office at Greenpeace USA's headquarters.

By the end of our first year, we had two Fortune 500 customers, Whole Foods and Staples. In our second year, we added two more major customers, IKEA and the State of California, and annual revenue broke $1 million. This success was unprecedented, as was all the work we were doing at the time.

The work was hard because, in every sense, we were doing something that nobody had ever done before. Certainly the third-party ownership structure had been done, but it was not widely known, and it had not been applied successfully to solar energy. Every bit of data that we put into the first spreadsheet model had to be validated when there was very little from which to draw additional information.

An example? Well, take "residual value." I put forth a proposed number that was key to model, but, when challenged, I had to go research to find data supporting the fact that solar panels would have value after twenty years. What did I find? A data set of eight transactions where used solar panels were resold. Hardly conclusively or scientifically sound but data nonetheless. We published white papers to validate our assertions, and so it went. With almost every aspect of the model, we had to prove and reprove our theory.

In 2005, two years after launch, we moved to a larger office space in Baltimore, our revenue jumped to close to $10 million, and we were growing at the rate of 1,000 percent per year. And we hadn't even worked out the kinks. One of my cofounders joked that we were growing faster than Amazon.com had in its early years.

By 2007, SunEdison employed six hundred people, and revenue catapulted to $200 million; we were growing at an unprecedented rate in a still-nascent industry. Five years later, in 2012, revenue at SunEdison solar was almost $2 billion, according to friends within SunEdison, now a subsidiary of Missouri-based MEMC Electronic Materials.

SunEdison was on the map. I had proven my hypothesis to myself, skeptics, and an impressive lineup of A-rated global players. But I wasn't satisfied. I had made my point, but the real work, convincing the world about the untapped power of solar, still lies ahead—which brings us back to why I am writing this book. We have validated that the model we created will work, but there are industry-level and government-level decisions that must be made to support continued growth and success if we are going to have an impact.

In 2003, the global solar industry was hovering around $5 billion; today it is $93 billion, proving again that my hypothesis about solar was creating wealth around the world.

How SunEdison Created a New and Better Business Model

SunEdison had a vision, but, we, like most entrepreneurial teams, had no idea what we were doing. In 2003, when we signed a contract with Whole Foods, we modified an existing energy services contract. Then we used that same contract with subsequent customers. The problem was that the contract was not really financeable.

When Goldman Sachs funded us in 2005, they rewrote much of our contract. Separately, Goldman Sachs used debt from Hudson United

Bank. Hudson United Bank had a lawyer (we later hired him) who checked every one of our documents before the bank would allow projects to be funded.

By 2006, we were no longer slowed down by paperwork; we were slowed down by the fact that outsourced contractors gave their own project priority over ours at SunEdison. As a result, we couldn't manage the timeline. So we merged a solar installer into SunEdison.

It was also a turning point for the business. We decided to have a razor sharp focus only on service model sales. So, we actually stopped selling systems requiring upfront costs and financing by the buyer. And, if you remember, upfront costs were a pain point for buyers I discovered early in my career.

The ending of cash sales and only selling "Solar as a Service" was actually a heated discussion and a bumpy transition. First, I remember when we made that decision. It was hard to get consensus and at some point we frankly had to overrule half of the management team.

Second, telling potential customers we didn't want to sell solar and make easy profits to ease our burden was painful but we had to focus – we were changing an industry. How painful was it? At that point, we weren't really profitable yet and almost couldn't make payroll.

However, with the decision made, everyone from the cash sales division was reassigned and trained to specialize. It was like we were a Henry Ford Assembly line. Everyone had their job and they got so good at it that they became experts.

The company bolted from the gate, and, to this day, no company in the still-emerging solar industry has come close. SunEdison not only set records, it created the paradigms for the industry's continued growth— a new, accessible, financially feasible way to finance and launch solar installations on a large scale.

In fact, our version 32 contract is still the one most plagiarized by law firms around the world. No one in the world has a specialized back office to analyze deals. It simply costs too much money to set up and so everyone else opts for generalists that aren't experts and make mistakes that are expensive to double-check.

And from inception, all the critical variables assuring continued success were working in our favor. By our third year, SunEdison was North America's largest solar service provider.

By our fourth year, people stopped cursing the solar services agreement we set up and started figuring out how to copy it. Today, 90 percent of all of the residential and commercial solar volume in the United States have their origins from our solar services agreement. We got there through focus. SunEdison almost died trying but humility and passion carried us through.

A key point to note is that everything that made SunEdison succeed was about business structure and not technology. The technology existed, we simply needed the right business model to get it adapted. You will see this theme again and again throughout this book.

Why the Rapid Growth?

Palming it off to luck borders on insult. In the big, bad, take-no-prisoners world of big business, you make your own luck, as the saying goes. More appropriately, Ray Kroc, McDonald's founder and creator of one of the most famous brands of all time, hit the proverbial nail on the head when he said: "Luck is a dividend of sweat. The more you sweat, the luckier you get."

We were sweating every waking hour making SunEdison successful. But fortuitous timing and unexplainable gut instinct certainly played a part in putting us on the global map.

Selling companies on solar wasn't difficult. By the time I started working the phones pitching solar, potential customers had already been pitched by at least five other solar companies. We didn't introduce them to solar, and we didn't have to convince them it was the smart thing to do. They already knew it made sense. The CFOs we spoke to just didn't want to spend $500,000 on a solar system; they'd rather spend it on opening new stores. The problem was they didn't know how to buy solar within their approved framework. SunEdison showed them how to do it. We offered them a more ingenious way to go solar. CFOs didn't want to spend their own cash on solar. And why should they? We said we would pay the $500,000 for the solar system and just charge them for the electricity, the same thing they were doing with the utility companies.

I quickly discovered that getting customers, whether prestigious, household-name companies or small, successful ones, wasn't difficult. More important was going deep with existing customers by adding more store and warehouse locations. Rather than having fifty customers with two stores and a warehouse, it made more sense to have five customers and do twenty stores and warehouse locations for each one.

Why? It was because we were providing a complex service that required many levels of approval, which included CFOs, lawyers, energy managers, facilities managers, landlords, government, and, most importantly, the investment-banking community.

Once we went through this rigorous, tedious process, it was a lot easier working with customers who had gone through it rather than trying to teach new customers the process.

Not Luck—Timing

There is a great truth in the hundreds of quotes about the importance and mystery of good timing. The right timing has meant success for thousands of products and services. The wrong timing has meant failure for the same number of products and services that potentially could have changed and improved the world.

Fortunately, the timing was right for SunEdison. SunEdison's success was based on the premarketing work of many US firms and the momentum created by other countries. Germany and Japan were investing significantly in solar and making a lot of money in the process. All this money movement got people in the investment-banking community watching and monitoring the emerging solar market.

Investment and finance organizations' decision-makers were impressed, as they should have been. Dollar signs were streaming across their hyperactive brains faster than Associated Press news feed reporting a breaking story.

The investment and finance people came to a conclusion I had arrived at a decade earlier: solar could make billions of dollars—and that was a lowball estimate. That's because oil and other commodities were getting more expensive; the modern energy crisis was upon us.

Each year, the solar industry was looking more attractive because it was growing at a phenomenal rate. It was more attractive to people in 2005 than it was in 2004, proving that there was great truth in the reassuring notion that the rising tide would lift all boats.

Deregulation of Electric-Utility Industry Spurs Growth of Solar

Between 1960 and 2000, electricity rates increased by about 0.6 percent a year, less than the cost of inflation. By the late 1990s, electricity prices catapulted, following Enron's spearheading deregulation of the electric-utility industry.

From 2000 to 2008, electricity prices for commercial customers went up about 4 percent a year, which was about seven times faster than expected. That translated to an extraordinary opportunity for SunEdison. We offered potential customers predictably priced solar with no upfront cost. By 2005, they started listening to us because they had experienced five years of an unexpected and unprecedented jump in their electric costs—irrefutable proof that timing is everything.

During this period, solar rode a high tide, not just in the United States but also in Germany, Japan, and other countries.

More importantly, George W. Bush decided solar photovoltaic (PV) was ready for a boost and increased the federal tax credit for solar PV from 10 to 30 percent. We closed our fund with Goldman Sachs in June 2005, two months before the George Bush Energy Policy Act passed—how's that for timing? The result: policies supporting solar were suddenly popular. It was no surprise to me; if you hate your utility company, the only option you have for local generation is solar—that, and the cost of solar was becoming very competitive.

A New and Better Energy Age

Based on the pragmatic concept of distributed generation, SunEdison paved the way for a new business paradigm, heralding the beginning of a new energy age. By putting solar power at the point of use—installing solar units on Wal-Mart and Staples rooftops, for example, rather than building solar plants in the middle of the desert—we avoided the need to bother with heavily contested transmission and distribution. Equally important, solar provided peak daytime electricity load when air conditioners were in full use and electricity costs were high, saving utility customers on their electricity bills. Once Wal-Mart got a taste for solar, they installed fuel cells, advanced energy efficiency, and even wind turbines in their parking lot.

Little Competition

Even though a new and very profitable marketplace was emerging, SunEdison had little competition. Each year, about two competitors tried to grab a piece of this market. But they lacked discipline and an understanding of customers' needs. And if they managed to get a piece of it, they were woefully ill equipped to hold on to it. For entrepreneurs focused on business model innovation this is always a place of great anxiety. Business model innovation is always about execution. We just focused on execution and outmaneuvered the "me too" companies trying to copy our business model.

No sooner did two competitors shut down than two more took their place, until they were forced to bow out because they didn't stand a chance of convincing institutional capital investment firms to give them money.

While a lot of people were selling and installing solar installations, few were offering solar as a service and saying to potential customers, "I'll pay for the power plant; you just pay me every month for the electricity you use."

Competitors failed because they didn't understand our business model: make the investors comfortable at all costs. Even if they grasped the concept, they didn't have the patience to endure the lengthy process.

To deliver what SunEdison was offering—solar as a service—a company has to gain the respect of investors. Convincing such customers as Staples and Kohl's was much easier than making Goldman Sachs and Wells Fargo happy. This requires a complete mind-shift. The customer is not just the rooftop owner but also the finance provider. As I stressed in Chapter 1, there is a pattern here most people don't understand. There are rules and strategies to this new approach to entrepreneurial projects.

There Are No Quick Fixes

And there are no shortcuts. In our early, critical years, we worked hard establishing strong relationships with some of the largest banks in the nation: Goldman Sachs, Wells Fargo, HSH Nordbank, Bank of Hawaii, and others. Goldman Sachs was the first, signing a $60-million commitment in June 2005. Once Goldman gave us the equivalent of the Good Housekeeping Seal of Approval, the other banks followed. It was as fundamental as, "If Goldman Sachs thinks SunEdison knows what it's doing then solar power must be a solid and profitable place to park our money."

Goldman's backing gave us instant credibility in the investment community. But for anyone who has ever worked with Goldman Sachs, that was not easy money. It was expensive and the hardest money out there. The fact that we saw that challenge as an opportunity to distance ourselves from competitors instead of taking the easier road was a big and important decision. The smart money is always hard, but in the end it is worth getting money from them vs. people perceived to be "soft" impact investors.

Each Success Was a Notch on Our Belt

Nothing in life is easy. Anything that is worthwhile requires sweat equity, stress, and all-consuming commitment. I figured this out soon after I stepped into the ring in 2003, and so did the tight group of committed people who worked with me. I didn't have to tell them what to expect. They knew it as soon as they signed on. For our first two years in business, SunEdison was going to be their lives. If they were putting in sixteen-hour days, in the remaining eight hours they were thinking or dreaming about getting things done. Looking back, our involvement with SunEdison was nothing short of obsessive. Okay, and maybe a little nuts, too. How different were we from all other entrepreneurial multibillion-dollar companies? Probably not much different, but at the time I remember thinking that we were working harder, smarter, and with more passion that anyone else. Well ... and maybe with a little too much undeserved confidence.

Everyone who played a critical part in SunEdison's launch fully understood the unspoken rules and project mission. We all knew that nothing short of total commitment would put SunEdison on the map. That's what it took to take my hypothesis from a one-dimensional idea to a business entity employing hundreds of people.

The Value of Doing It the Hard Way

The big banks weren't looking for one-hit wonders. They were all about building long, sustainable relationships. And to build those relationships, we had to run the gauntlet—not once, but over and over again.

What we were doing was hard. It involved a complex and lengthy process. But early on we learned the importance of respecting the order of things. We represented business model innovation. Mainstream banks are stubborn. They had a process and no amount coaxing from us would convince them to relax it for us because it worked for them. So we learned every step and didn't question it – at least for the first few years.

Our initial competitors felt they could sidestep the process—find shortcuts, an easier way. They felt they could find impact investors who believed in solar. When I was asked for advice about taking this path, my response was this: "Sure, why not? You can do that. But impact investors don't scale."

As for going the banking route as we did, the truth is big banks are difficult and frustrating to work with; they ask hundreds of questions because they're constantly trying to figure out how they're going to be screwed. As stressful as it was, I resigned myself to the process. We had no choice but to answer the unending barrage of questions. When we thought we satisfied all their requirements, they found more questions to ask. Or they'd ask me to write a white paper about the residual value of solar panels or what the Kelly Blue Book value of solar panels would be in five years or prepare a credit model about what was going to happen over the next twenty years to our customers because the contracts were twenty-years long. It didn't matter to them that we didn't know how to do a credit model. We had to figure it out. There was no light at the end of the tunnel. They just kept on asking us more questions until they were satisfied with the answers. They didn't say, "Just bear with us another four months; we guarantee that you'll get through it." Instead, they'd say, "We didn't like your answers. We need more information."

Most of our competitors didn't want to go through this rigorous, tedious process. For good reason.

The reality was the banks were making it hard for us. But there was no other way to do it. If we cheated and took money from a high-net-worth individual, our model wouldn't scale.

It's not that the banks were going out of their way to be difficult, sadistically putting us through a tortuous process. Their job was to thoroughly understand every transaction. To accomplish this, the evaluation process ranged from six to twelve months.

Unlike many mature businesses where there is a checklist of requirements, solar was new—to everyone. There were no checklists because the banks and law firms were making them up on the fly. A $1.1-million legal bill and 8 months later, we finally got the Goldman Sachs deal done.

Change Is Possible

The upside to this frustrating, seemingly endless due-diligence process is that we had someone on the other side who thought we were worth working with and who was willing to shepherd us through the process. We were learning on the job; each experience prepared us for the next bank. When a bank said it wanted to work with us, we already had all the documents we created for the last bank. So we dumped all the documents on the new bank, hoping to accelerate the process and make it easier for the bank and us. Yet every bank we worked with had a law firm that wanted to prove how smart it was and how much it could run up the bill. They weren't looking to standardize the process.

But the big lesson is that change is achievable, and we proved that it is possible. We proved to the investment community, banks, government, and industry that a new energy infrastructure is possible. We opened a new door for other entrepreneurs, demonstrating that there are new, exciting, and untapped business opportunities.

But there are no quick fixes, and there are no shortcuts, only a badly sketched treasure map to new destinations. Along the way, several of our board members left to start a new fund and created a competitor to us. But we had to play by their rules because that was the way things were done. Again, there were no shortcuts, no getting around the process.

Good Work Brings Its Own Just Rewards

Word got out in the finance community about our company because they all speak to one another at conferences. The project financing community was so small that there were only fifty to a hundred project finance experts in the whole country. When you have such a small community, having a reference like Goldman Sachs goes a long way. These folks are generally not the highest earners in the bank. They are low-risk folks who invest in people that are referred to them.

Keep in mind that the finance community's job is to put money to work. It's not to say no. If they rejected every project, they'd be making 2-percent interest on their money in US Treasury bonds. So they had to say yes to someone. They discovered that we were a good place to put their money. It's not that they didn't want to give us money. But to get it, we had to sweat and keep the gatekeepers happy. If we failed to do so, they wouldn't cut us a check.

Yes, it's a long, hard road conquering that check, but in the final analysis, it's worth every tedious, anxious, tormenting moment. Today, global consultants McKinsey & Company and the International Energy Agency believe that the solar industry is on track to put $1 trillion to work by 2020. Not all of that is because of SunEdison, but we were an influential piece of it. Acceptance by global finance is part of the process. Now that the deals have been consummated, and I put the ordeal in perspective, I not only understand the process, but I also respect it. The process works. And that's all that matters.

Section II:
The Lessons

CHAPTER FOUR:

I Didn't Start SunEdison to Make Money

Defining Entrepreneurship

Entrepreneurs are a breed unto themselves. And there is no shortage of definitions for the word—along with thousands of articles and hundreds of books explaining entrepreneurship in tedious detail. Do the mere definitions do the term, and the individuals, justice?

The word's origin can be traced to the French word *entreprendre*, which means "to undertake," and nineteenth-century French economist Jean-Baptiste Say coined it. In his book, *A Treatise on Political Economy,* Say defined an entrepreneur as "one who undertakes an enterprise, especially a contractor, acting as intermediary between capital and labor" (Say, 1855).

The US Small Business Administration tersely describes an entrepreneur as "a person who organizes and operates a business, usually with considerable initiative, while taking on greater than normal financial risk in order to do so" (SBA, 2013).

Roy Ash, cofounder of Litton Industries, describes an entrepreneur as "someone who bites off a little more than he can chew hoping he'll quickly learn how to chew it" (Ash, 2013).

"The entrepreneur builds an enterprise; the technician builds a job," says business writer Michael Gerber (Ferris, 2008).

"An entrepreneur is focused on innovation, such as new products, new production methods, new markets, and new forms of organization," according to Austrian economist Joseph Schumpeter (Hagedoorn, 1985).

Missing the Point

I won't belabor the definitions, all of which are a variation on the creation of an enterprise that makes a lot of money. Most of the definitions of "entrepreneur" woefully miss the point.

Coming from an entrepreneurial family, and after talking to and observing entrepreneurs as far back as I can remember, I have a different take on what defines an entrepreneur. Contrary to popular opinion, successful entrepreneurs, regardless of industry, share a common trait: *they are focused on solving real problems rather than making money.* They start businesses because they want to solve problems that people are willing to pay to have them solve. And if the problems are of sufficient scale, entrepreneurs can become very wealthy.

There is an erroneous notion that most entrepreneurs launch businesses because they are convinced that starting a business is a great way to make money. Unquestionably, entrepreneurship can be a vehicle to enormous wealth. Yet I don't know any entrepreneurs who started their businesses for that reason. Furthermore, entrepreneurship is not easy, and it is certainly not a low-risk way to achieve wealth.

The Quest for Solutions

That foundation-building approach of starting a business by searching for a solution to a problem can be applied to any business—from a dry cleaner, donut shop, or bicycle-repair shop to a clothing factory, auto or computer manufacturer, or nationwide discount-grocery chain.

Take the entrepreneur who wants to open a restaurant, for example. There is no shortage of restaurants, but the smart restaurateur lays the foundation for his or her business by asking a question: "Is there a need, a strong demand, for this type of restaurant?" Then he or she sets out to answer that question. The restaurateur searches for a solution to the problem by asking smart and objective people. He or she hopes to discover that there is a demand for the cuisine the restaurant plans to offer. If he or she is right, the restaurant can solve a problem by filling a gap, and if the restaurateur goes about focusing on all the details to meeting this unmet need, he or she stands to be successful.

Prove Hypothesis beyond a Reasonable Doubt

A critical step dictating success or failure is testing and proving a hypothesis beyond a reasonable doubt. The operative words in that last sentence are "beyond a reasonable doubt."

This process can be likened to debating yourself about a controversial issue. You are arguing, disputing, and questioning every variable and factor playing into the success or failure of your hypothesis. If all entrepreneurs subjected themselves to this type of intense questioning and analysis before they thought about writing a business plan and finding office space, there would be fewer business fatalities each year.

The hypothesis "one day the whole world will be powered by solar," the foundation for launching SunEdison, consumed me. It was like a powerful magnet pulling me to information that either confirmed or debunked my assertion. For almost a decade, it propelled and energized me most of my waking hours. I couldn't gather enough information on the subject. Throughout my information quest, I kept asking myself questions such as these: "What is the best way, strategy, or method for gathering information?" "Where am I going to find it?" "How am I going to evaluate my sources?" And once all the information would be gathered, "How do I objectively evaluate it?"

It's not a simple process by any stretch of the imagination.

Immerse Yourself in the Process

The importance of investing time and thought into this discovery process is not to be underestimated. It can be done in different ways. The best approach is to pursue the hypothesis objectively and pragmatically. As much as entrepreneurs want encouragement, they also know how important it is to dredge up dissenters, naysayers, people who will debunk the hypothesis. It doesn't matter what their motives are—whether dissenters steadfastly believe their reasons are valid or whether they're part of the competition and just don't want entrepreneurs to find solutions supporting the hypothesis is irrelevant. The entrepreneur must be able to refute objections as a test to the hypothesis.

Supporters, especially colleagues and friends who share your beliefs, are easy to find. But listening to them is a terrible way to test a business premise because the information you're getting is biased, subjective, and self-serving.

Others, like me, purposely take the hard path, walk into the lion's den, and seek out people who will shout them down and aggressively reject their assumptions. It's not a pleasant or comfortable road to take, but it's the only one likely to deliver information from sources that are either unbiased or biased against you.

By the same token, it can be a tormenting process that could have a bad outcome.

In my own case, after years of research and analysis, I risked learning that my hypothesis was flawed and full of holes and wasn't worth pursuing. I can't imagine what that discovery would have felt like. I'm thankful I never found out.

A related hypothesis about solar was that distributed generation would be successful. To test it, I spent one hundred dollars to post the hypothesis on the website Longbets.com. I did it so people would argue with me and challenge my hypothesis.

And they did, proving that it was worth every penny getting that feedback. It demonstrated how important it is to have your hypothesis clear and clean enough so it can be challenged. If it's ambiguous, you're not doing yourself any good by avoiding criticism.

This is why I rigorously tested myself and went to great lengths to find people who would give me productive feedback. I wanted them to be brutally honest and say, "I don't think your hypothesis is feasible because it's hard to raise money." Or, "The probability of succeeding is very slight because of these factors or issues." Or, "What you're trying to do is impossible because of the science or market factors."

Typically, one question triggers more questions and objections. During this learning process, I discovered that some people had legitimate reasons for debunking my hypothesis, opening another learning door. If there are roadblocks, I want to know about them early on.

There is great truth in the startup axiom "fail fast." If you're going down a dead-end road, and there is no sign of an alternate path, abort. Don't fail after you've wasted $10 million of someone else's money. These are reasons enough to first make sure your hypothesis is crystal clear, so it can be challenged, tested, and proven beyond a reasonable doubt.

This process is the critical starting point for most high-growth entrepreneurs. They start their businesses by looking at all the variables that determine success or failure. If they go about the process meticulously, they'll probably conclude—even if they discover unforeseen barriers—that problems can be overcome and that their business is worth launching.

The farsighted entrepreneurs who changed and shaped our world tested their business premises in a similar way.

The seeds of Econet Wireless, for example, were planted when founder Strive Masiyiwa thought that twenty-two phone connections for every thousand people in Africa was a human rights violation. While considering how to solve this gap through the existing monopoly phone company, he concluded that only a competitor using a leapfrog technology could work. This is obvious today, but, at the time, Masiyiwa had to win his case at the Zimbabwe Supreme Court under the presidency of Robert Mugabe. His hypothesis was that telecommunication was a fundamental right for which people would pay.

Testing and proving he could do it made Masiyiwa a groundbreaking pioneer who helped to usher in a new era on the continent of Africa. Access to mobile phones has been responsible for most of the economic progress in local development in the past twenty years in Africa.

Michael Haas started Orion Renewable Energy Group, which focuses on wind energy. Haas saw that wind was fundamentally easier to develop than large coal plants and that very few people wanted to do the tough prospecting work necessary to find the right wind sites. He raised high-risk capital to find and develop these sites and eventually sold his company to British Petroleum, who wanted to deploy wind power without the development risk. Today, hundreds of companies in wind, solar, geothermal, hydro, and other renewable electricity technologies have copied this model—having seen the enormous profits that can be earned from solving a problem.

There are hundreds of examples of entrepreneurial hypotheses that have been the foundation for multibillion-dollar companies. History has repeatedly proven that entrepreneurial creativity is fueled by market dynamics and changing economies. In his blog, *Dispatches from the New World of Work*, management consultant, author, and speaker Tom Peters wrote, "Entrepreneurial capitalism is the strongest force possible for unleashing human potential."

Understand Your Customers

When I launched SunEdison, I had to find the right set of perfect customers—the right early adopters—to prove my hypothesis and drive the growth of the company. I had to identify them and avoid global statements and generalizations about them. I discovered that the market is composed of concentric circles. There were customers who were right at the moment, and there were others who weren't.

When you are a young company, the "right" customers know that you are early and cut you some slack. So many entrepreneurs I meet are intent on closing Wal-Mart as their first client. That is usually impossible. Why? Because when you have no money, they still won't budge an inch. They won't give you better terms or relax their requirements. Some customers will and those are the ones you want to start with. It doesn't mean that Wal-Mart wouldn't be right later on. Each time you close the right customer, you have the right to expand to the next concentric circle – a slightly more demanding but manageable customer.

It is important in this model to understand the value of reference customers. These are customers whose name has enough clout to reinforce or underscore the value of the service you provide. This clout must impress other future potential customers as well as your investors. It is, after all, a three-way negotiation: you, customers and funders.

The hope is that attracting the right customers will lead to investors saying they will take another look. It is important to understand this and be strategic in the business you select. In our case, we did turn away some early leads or potential customers. That seems unthinkable, but, strategically, they were not right for us at the time. What we found out, however, was that being honest and straightforward with them from the beginning helped a great deal, and they understood why we made the choices we did.

I had to measure success a certain way so that SunEdison sustained rapid growth. To accomplish that, my initial goals had to be attainable. That first set of customers opened doors to new customers, creating new market comfort points, thus broadening my reach and strengthening my credibility.

Without that credibility, I never would have been able to close Wal-Mart, for example. Wal-Mart valued the stability that solar provided for their volatile electricity rates. The fact that the company had a green halo from solar was good, but it wasn't going to pay a premium for that halo. When I initially pitched them, Wal-Mart executives said, "Jigar, we know you can make one hundred rooftops cost-effective, but unless you can make it work across one thousand, we don't want to talk to you."

In order to prove my hypothesis, experience taught me how important it was to work with the right customers at the right time. In that crucial startup period, SunEdison's line of ascent was drawn customer by customer—one proof point to the next. The hard part was seeing and understanding how each new customer would lead to the next.

It matters who your first customers are because they set an important precedent for the future. Prove your hypothesis in a way that allows you to work to scale. Whole Foods, Staples, and the State of California were marquee names that encouraged Goldman Sachs to finance our first $60-million project fund. It was not until 2006 that we went after Wal-Mart to sign virtually the same contract that Staples signed in 2003. In fact, Wal-Mart ended up paying a higher price because, in this kind of business, it pays to be the first customer.

Recognizing the need for the right customers and sticking to the principle of finding that marquee business requires discipline. The business did not fall into our laps. We worked hard through our networks to get in to speak with the right people and then worked through the connections until we got in front of the right decision-makers. Those first reference customers are worth waiting for and working for. You will work just as hard to support a customer with no reference value or name recognition. It makes sense to invest your time on the front end to attract business that will lead to more business.

We also learned early on that the project investors were in charge. We did not offer a lot of concessions from one customer to the next, but we were mindful of the risk of a one-size-fits-all approach. We worked closely with our customers from the beginning and adjusted according to their needs but were always mindful of the project investors' requirements. From the original contract in 2003 to the final contract with which I was involved in 2008, our "standard agreement" had undergone thirty-two official revisions.

Engineering Matters

SunEdison's contractors had to satisfy each customer's specific needs, which meant choosing the appropriate solar technology. There are twenty solar panel manufacturers with good reputations, ten different inverter manufacturers (which convert variable direct-current output of photovoltaic solar panels into utility-frequency alternating current that can be fed into commercial electrical grids), and forty different mounting structures, not to mention all of the other variables.

Even though SunEdison was largely a finance play, and I'm not an R&D expert, it was critical that we knew how to evaluate technology; we weren't just providing financing and contracting services. Like all our customers, Staples expected us to review all the solar possibilities out there and recommend the best one. They asked us questions, expected us to have the right answers, and trusted us to provide the best possible service.

In the consumer space, for example, there are times it doesn't matter that a customer isn't pleased with a product even though the company made performance claims. The customer will never come back if they are dissatisfied, and the company still gets paid.

It's a different story in the infrastructure space. Every variable in the relationship is important because customers sign service contracts, which they expect to be honored to the letter. If the contracts are not honored, the customer simply stops paying. Customers want to be assured that the equipment will work well enough to achieve the savings they were promised. This is not only true for solar but for transportation, clean water, controlled environment agriculture, or virtually any infrastructure. Making fanciful claims based upon lab test results not only won't fly but may also get you into trouble quickly. Customers want to know that the equipment they purchase from us will work in real-world conditions.

It's important to have technological expertise, to understand how every facet of a system works, so we can predict how our decisions will affect the customer.

Technology Can't Save the World

SunEdison is about business model and finance innovation. A lot of people out there really want to believe that technology will save the world. But people who live in the infrastructure world know that technology is rarely the differentiator.

Engineering, finance, operational excellences are all reliable differentiators in the infrastructure space. Technology can't save the world because decision-makers won't let it. The reason solar was at $93 billion in 2011 is because there it had been around in its current form since the 1970s – that's a long track record with technology differentiators. Infrastructure is supposed to be boring. Unlike the technology markets with singular, dominant players offering universal solutions, in infrastructure, there is no place for an all-knowing Apple computer.

Infrastructure decision-makers expect there to be a minimum of a ten – to twenty-year track record for the solutions they implement. Anything less and you are still in the "pilot" phase. And, most often, a solution involves multiple component players because the playing field is exceedingly complex.

In the end, as unimportant as technology may be, entrepreneurs have to keep up with new stuff—investors and customers depend on you to be the expert. Equally important, they must also learn to trust their guts—infrastructure has to be profitable for an extended period of time. Which incremental technologies could help improve profitability without scaring investors and customers?

Financial Resources That Deliver Real-World Results

In the infrastructure space, the rule of Mesopotamian commerce holds true. I provide a service; you pay me. After I pay my debts, I hope there is money left over, which is my profit. The logic may be simplistic, but it makes sense because that's what building a successful business is all about. You can't make excuses for not getting the basics right.

Fundamentally, if you're going to build the impact economy, you have to build companies that actually produce cash flow. To survive and, more importantly, to grow, a company must sustain a profitable income. Dozens of companies bit the dust during the dot-com era because they believed that "eyeballs" were enough to sustain unprofitable momentum.

In a similar fashion in the clean-tech era, many companies continue to raise money on the promise that they have the game-changing technology that will displace the current leaders. If you have to keep raising money from investors until you work out your financial issues, you're in serious trouble. Raising money to achieve higher volumes when your unit economics—the amount of money you make on each sale—is negative is just plain insanity.

SunEdison's situation was solid. We made money on every project. We had to keep raising money from investors because we were growing rapidly and needed more working capital to sustain our growth. But on a unit-by-unit economics basis, we were making money. That's what defined our success.

If you expect to make it as an entrepreneur, you can't define success through a new-age metric. It always comes down to money—you are either generating it or consuming it.

Manage Change—Expect the Unexpected

No matter how meticulously you plan every move, things will go awry. More often than not, changes will happen suddenly, without warning. It's often when you think you've reached a plateau, and everything is going better than expected. Why? Because shit happens.

If you are not primed for the unexpected, you are not running your business well. If you naïvely believe that everything has to go right for your company to be successful, you're going to fail. You have to be open-minded and know that unexpected problems will arise.

Early on, we learned that solar problems could occur at practically any part of the installation process, stressing the necessity of having a contingency plan to quickly resolve them.

Successful entrepreneurs respect Murphy's Law, which says that if anything can go wrong, it will. Don't try to analyze it or overthink it; just react quickly, solve the problem, and get on with business. Dealing with unexpected crises only makes you faster, smarter, and a better manager.

What Drives Great Entrepreneurs?

Summing up, David Skok, serial entrepreneur and a partner in venture-capital firm Matrix Partners, simply explains entrepreneurial success as follows: "In the startup world, if your primary focus is on making money, you usually won't make money. When you work because you are passionate about your work, I believe you maximize your chances of making money" (Skok, 2010).

It's never about money but rather an unshakable belief in solutions.

CHAPTER FIVE:

Respect the Sacred Rules of Mainstream Capital Investing

When I launched SunEdison, I believed that I could convince investors that solar power was a smart investment because it was considerably less risky than other energy projects. I thought I was arguing from a position of strength. I did my homework and prepared an ironclad presentation, full of facts, statistics, and projections, proving my hypothesis about solar.

You can't argue with the fact that solar has no moving parts, that the sun is free, and that solar can be produced where it is used—where it is most valuable. The amount of sun that hits a specific spot on earth varies by less than 4 percent each year. Solar is very stable and secure. Most importantly, solar can be deployed in bite-sized amounts, not by the billions of dollars needed to design, build, operate, and maintain power plants that run on coal or nuclear fission, not to mention the safety and health risks of those kinds of power.

Dwindling Energy Supplies

Then there is the issue of energy supply. Coal, oil, natural gas, and uranium are finite. Even if they don't run out soon, their costs will continue to go up as they become more expensive to find and to pull out of the ground. But the sun will be burning hot for at least another five billion years, scientists predict.

To support my assertions, I quoted Shimon Awerbuch, the high priest of energy economics who tragically and unexpectedly passed away in 2007. Awerbuch often questioned why investments in renewable-energy projects were expected to achieve the same high rates of return as natural gas and coal when gas and coal were riskier. Solar carries a much lower risk, he believed, more like a "savings bond." Once the equipment is paid for, the sun is free, and maintenance costs are low. He postulated that solar deserved a lower cost of capital in several works he published where he examined overall risk associated with various energy sources (Awerbach, 2007).

I approached banks, private-equity firms, and smaller investors with my research, thinking I was a shoo-in to receive backing at a low rate of return. I was wrong.

After I approached Goldman Sachs and gave them all my research, I thought they'd say: "You're absolutely right. We're going to give you a lot of money at six percent interest." Instead, they told me that the idea was very interesting, and they would have to crunch some numbers and get back to me.

I left thinking they'd offer very favorable terms. When they got back to me with a term sheet, they wanted 17 percent on their money. When I asked the obvious question, "Why seventeen percent?" they said, "We understand your thesis, but we still want our standard rate of return." They also pointed out that I wouldn't have come to them if I had a bunch of investors willing to give me 6-percent interest.

They were smart guys. I needed other interested investors.

It didn't take me long to sort it out. It's the law of supply and demand. I was the little guy on the block, and this is the way things work.

The Power of Mainstream Investing

The truth was that we did have other investors, but they were impact investors, not mainstream investors. One of my competitors raised money from a group of San Diego Charger football players and got them to invest at a much lower interest rate. My first thought was, *Oh, my God, I'm negotiating with Goldman Sachs at 17-percent interest, and my competitors are getting between 6-percent and 8-percent interest from a bunch of football players. What am I doing wrong?*

But when I gave it serious thought, I realized that once my competitors got their initial seed money, it would be unlikely that they would be able to come back and ask for more money. They couldn't count on an unlimited pot of money from sports figures. And professional football players investing in my competitors' companies didn't inspire mainstream investors such as Goldman Sachs. They didn't raise an eyebrow or think anything about it; in fact, they were unmoved by the competitor's ability to raise that money. The Goldman Sachs financial analysts doubted that the football players did their due diligence. They were probably right.

By going through the process required by Goldman Sachs, we were setting a precedent for ourselves as a high-caliber investment opportunity. This is critically important to future customers and to future investors. What this said about SunEdison is that we were not taking shortcuts or going the easiest route but rather creating an organization that could bear the scrutiny of the mainstream investment community and merit funding. To be clear, this is not getting easy money; it is the opposite, but it set us up for so much more success down the road. Easy money leads to bad habits and does not scale.

The Complexities of Impact Investing

The people who are investing in impact companies are doing it for the right reasons. They want to make an impact first and a decent rate of return second. They have split their attention between both making an impact and determining the right risk—the adjusted rate of return. However, their split due diligence efforts often gives short shift to the finance side of the process. This is important to understand. The average impact investor, for example, will ask general questions, such as: "Are you improving the environment? What is the impact on climate change? How many jobs will you create locally? Is most of the equipment locally manufactured?"

Large, prestigious investment-banking firms aren't impressed with most impact investors because their criteria for measuring success are wildly different. After sweating the long and tedious evaluation process, I understood why Goldman Sachs analyzes every investment, especially the financials. It's not easy figuring out the right tough questions for a new asset class. It's even harder asking tough questions about impact. SunEdison represented both of these things and therefore required a different level of scrutiny. Once we passed that test, however, we recognized the enormity of our potential both for future customers and investors for having gone through the process as we did.

The Goldman Sachs finance people are very well trained, and they look at an increasingly complex and ever-changing big picture; they know what they are doing. They not only can do the due diligence part of the financing process well, but they are also on the lookout for such things as toxic building materials, energy returned on energy invested, and sustainable policy. On the surface, a company may appear to be making an impact with a product such as fertilizers, but the same technique that helps thousands of African farmers produce more food could be polluting rivers and streams and the livelihood of thousands of fishermen.

It is important to understand how the questions change when we are working in five villages versus an entire country. The difference between micro impact and macro impact creates intricacies within impact investing that make it difficult to figure out if something that you are investing $1,000 into at the village level is still a good investment at a larger level.

Practically speaking, the truth is that in the traditional markets the finance side of an impact investment actually matters more. The future looms in the distance as an unfathomable unknown. Everything looks good right now, but what happens if there is a financial crisis like the one we had in 2008? When we pitched Goldman Sachs, we weren't facing a financial crisis. But I'm sure Goldman's finance team was factoring unknown variables into their analysis of SunEdison's long-term outlook. No one knows what lies ahead, but they had to consider all possibilities in order to make a smart long-term investment choice.

There is this notion of many politicians and voters that if something is good for the planet and society, it should be subsidized and carry low interest rates. I do not agree. The problem is that when interest rates are low, investors invest only to feel good, not because they are taking the time to actually understand the asset class. Over time, this is not helpful to the industries that are trying to grow because funding is inconsistent. Smart investors know the importance of making good money as the leader and have other investors follow by attaching their brand to a new, underappreciated asset class. It's the way the game is played.

An Imperfect Game

The rules governing mainstream investing are always changing. They reflect the unpredictable winds of changing economies. Investors must adjust their investment requirements to the economic conditions of the moment. Inflation and other risk factors can suddenly change investment parameters. What may appear to be a solid investment could quickly turn into a bad investment if inflation suddenly jumps to 10 percent. In the wake of the 2008 financial crisis, many investors moved their portfolios to ultra-low-risk investments, but they couldn't do that for long because people have such high expectations on return. The tough part is trying to understand all the components of the investing puzzle and figuring out which pieces they represent. Today, investments such as renewable energy represent low-risk ways of making much higher returns than real estate investment trusts (REITs) or other dividend funds.

The game isn't perfect, but, rest assured, investors of all types—from individuals to fund managers to bankers—need to put their money to work just as badly as we need the money to make a difference in the world. History has proven that, while flawed, capitalism works—most of the time.

Not All Investment Capital Is the Same

Why choose impact-investing capital over mainstream capital? Knowing we can't really change the world at gigaton scale without $100 billion to $2 trillion in investments per sector, why choose impact-investing capital over mainstream capital? That's a tough question entrepreneurs struggle to answer.

There is a ridiculous notion that every good deed is worth doing, articulately encapsulated by the starfish story. A boy on the beach throws starfish one by one back into the ocean. When asked how he could possibly save all of the starfish, he responds, "I made a difference to this starfish." One person throwing starfish into the ocean doesn't matter unless several thousand people follow that person's lead. In infrastructure, that means the world can't be changed without at least $100 billion in investments. And if that's what it takes, the question is, how do we reach that scale?

Consensus thinking says the first task is testing the deployment of the technology, so pilot projects are all that matter. It doesn't matter what kind of capital is used, whether it is grant money or concessional loan money that expects just 4-percent interest, as long as we know that the pilot was successful by getting the technology out there with good results.

The problem with that approach is that we don't understand the risks associated with these investments and what the interest rates should be.

Look at it this way: if someone said, "This investment is amazing. It's a one-hundred-million-dollar bond offer to provide energy access for the poor in Kenya; we should buy them at ten-percent interest."

The problem is we have no way to know whether 10 percent is a good return. We don't have any qualms about bonds or supporting the company because it's doing something that makes the world a better place. The problem is that we know nothing about the quality of the bond. Is it rated highly, or is it a junk bond? What is the inflation rate in Kenya? Do you have the ability to change the price based on inflation?

In the private space, trusted, highly paid experts evaluate bonds and can tell us whether we're getting a good return. In the public space, respected investment-rating service companies, such as S&P and Moody's, rate bonds on a quality scale: AAA, AA-, BBB+, etc.

If those ratings aren't available, how do we know whether we made a smart investment call? If it turns out to be a good call, was it skill or luck?

The Critical Question from the Impact Investor's Perspective

Put yourself in an impact investor's shoes. As an illustration, imagine that you manage a fund that cares about outcomes. The return is important but not as important as making the world a better place in some way—helping people pull themselves out of poverty or providing clean water. In short, making a social impact.

The critical question is, can you make an impact without sacrificing your standards and your thresholds on the profit side? Right now, most people believe that impact investors sacrifice good due diligence on the finance side in exchange for better due diligence on the impact side. That's because they are more concerned with making an impact for their investors than with making sure it's really a good investment.

As long as this perception exists—whether true or not is irrelevant—mainstream investors are not going to follow these investors at a $100-billion scale.

If you really want to help people at scale then the work that you are doing with your fund, whether it's $2 million, $20 million, or $200 million, needs to represent a model that has extensive transparent research underlying and supporting its investment decisions, based on maximizing returns in a chosen sector. The research has to garner credibility and value. The research has to be so solid that other entrepreneurs plagiarize it, and mainstream investors are persuaded by it.

The Challenge

Here's another hypothetical example. You're an entrepreneur, and your first investment is rock-star quality. It's got a substantial government subsidy, and you've got a solid guarantee from the city that they are going to buy all of the output from your project.

Everything is going well. But now you're at a developmental crossroads calling for a critical decision. You can maximize profits by taking money from an impact investor who doesn't care about a high rate of return. Or you can go with a more respected investor who will want a higher rate of return, consequently lowering your profit margin. The value of the respected money is that it could set you up to get more money in the future.

Our hypothetical entrepreneur finds him- or herself in a strange place. In fact, a couple of companies I've funded have found themselves at that same uncertain crossroads. The entrepreneurs came to me asking for advice. They have said, "I got this offer for really cheap money."

My response? "I get it. But if you take it, it won't be any easier raising money the next time around." The challenge, therefore, is to have the discipline to take the long-term view and work with money that will help you to scale when you need more.

Make Smart Choices with Capital

To drive home the importance of choosing smart investment capital, as an example, I'll cite an infrastructure company in which I invested. The company is taking money from the Acumen Fund, which is actually an impact-investing fund. The company is taking money from Acumen because it is well known and respected. The company also gains access to more than 1,000 people for its network.

The questions the company faced were: "Is it worth taking money from Acumen?" and, "How will venture capitalists view it? Will they see it as a smart move? Or will they see it as a bad move and not want to invest in it?"

A great deal of thought went into going with Acumen. We decided that it was a smart move because, as an investor in the company, we would gain access to government programs and sponsors, all of which limit our risk.

In terms of project finance money, we deliberately went after smart, expensive capital, even though we could have increased profit by taking cheaper money. We did it so we can strategically position ourselves in order to attract much more money when the company's first project was completed. It was important for us to make sure that this first financing was substantive proof to mainstream investors that the company was worth looking at. This is the type of decision more entrepreneurs have to consider making if we are going to reach impact-level momentum in infrastructure. The long game for everyone is better when the technologies are successfully deployed, well respected by customers and investors, and scaled to meet the need.

Worth the Cost and Trouble

I can't offer panacea solutions, shortcuts to beat the system, or quick fix tips opening doors to the movers and shakers in the mainstream finance world. I'm sorry that I don't have any. And I doubt if they exist. Like me, entrepreneurs have to sweat a lot and jump through hoops to get the smart capital. Unquestionably, it's the hard road. But it's the right road if you really want to make a big difference—in fact, it's the only road.

Capital firms expect an extraordinary amount of transparency. They ask a lot of questions, and they expect a lot of answers. And if they're dissatisfied with the answers, they may pull out of financing your project.

But all that scrutiny and discipline teaches you to think like a mainstream capitalist. It helps you to understand why the mainstream capital market needs what it needs and why its representatives ask endless questions.

The first time high-potential entrepreneurs take money from impact investors, they most likely bypass this intense level of scrutiny. The downside is that they sidestep a priceless learning experience that they would have gotten had they gone after mainstream capital. When they get to a point where they need additional funding to grow, they're rarely prepared with the critical skills, due diligence, and data necessary to convince mainstream investors that they're a worthwhile investment. Over time, this greatly limits both their growth and their credibility.

Making an Impact

In the infrastructure space, the way you make an impact is by deploying millions of units. If you're in the clean water business, it will eventually take a $1-trillion investment to provide clean water to all those in the world who don't currently have it. For example, I have come across nonprofits dedicated to bringing clean water the world's poor, yet few are on track to raise that kind of money. To lay a strong foundation for the future, picking the right money partners and financial model early on is critical. Often, maximizing short-term profit doesn't lead to maximizing long-term profit. Unfortunately, many entrepreneurs heading high-potential companies lack the financial resources to make a significant impact because they fell into the cheap money trap and couldn't pull themselves out.

All investments have the potential to move toward an impact economy. Unfortunately, not all socially responsible investments will. Most won't.

Not to belabor the critical point of this chapter, but impact investing must have compelling returns that make professional investors consider them seriously as a critical piece in the portfolio. Dr. Arjuna Sittampalam, research associate with EDHEC-Risk Institute, succinctly captured the objective: "The investor makes an active decision to seek a social or developmental return alongside [the] financial return" (Sittampalam, 2011). It is this balance between the social benefit and the financial reward that must be maintained to correctly move toward an impact economy. It is that balance that will allow us to shift from incidents of SRIs to a movement that supports this investment model in markets around the world. The opportunity is vast, and the timing is right.

CHAPTER SIX:

The Role of Government

"We cannot cede to other nations the technology that will power new jobs and new industries. We must claim its promise."
—President Barack Obama, Inaugural Address, January 21, 2013

It is not practical to talk about tapping into the enormous climate wealth market that infrastructure represents without talking about the role of government. Even if there are no subsidies, government sets the rules and often has to provide permission in the form of permits.

For practical purposes, let's examine a real example in the United States. In 2012, President Obama was elected to a second term in office. Since his first election in 2008, the president has mentioned infrastructure as one way to get blue-collar workers back to work and America back to prominence. His approach so far has been to have EPA regulate pollutants and have Congress allocate money for projects. Still, there are many more things that he could do if he and his administration optimized how mainstream capital works.

There are enormous climate wealth opportunities and challenges in three areas worth noting: mobility (transportation), energy (electricity), and water. We need only look at the devastation after Hurricane Sandy to truly understand firsthand our extensive dependence on transportation, electricity, and water.

I am an entrepreneur, and I believe that the "controlled chaos" of free markets drives economic growth. Government is the control, and entrepreneurs create the chaos. To be clear, these are distinct roles. When government becomes a player—think about the investment into Solyndra, the solar panel manufacturer that went bankrupt after a $500-million-plus infusion of capital from the US government—it does not work. Yet government is needed if we are going to effect the necessary changes to drive climate wealth business growth and improvements in these sectors. And the sectors are too important not to have government oversight.

First and foremost, we need a plan. "All of the above" is not a plan. It is a recipe for confusion. It lacks the focus and clearly articulated goals that a plan entails and leaves too many questions unanswered. Government must be clear about what the priorities are when it comes to these essential areas so that everyone understands in which direction we are going. Imagine if we had built the US interstate system in the 1950s and 1960s without a government plan.

It is really essential that the government serve as a point of coordination—almost a fulcrum—for these efforts. In optimizing our climate wealth opportunities, infrastructure funders, governments, and key decision-makers are not yet all on board. This type of infrastructure development is complex and requires all the key players have consistent and equal participation at all times because any one of them can scuttle a deal. (This is why it is so complicated. No one side really has control.)

An example I cited in a *Fast Company* article was SEMATECH. Conceived in 1986, SEMATECH began operating in 1988 as a partnership between the US government and fourteen US-based semiconductor manufacturers. The goal of SEMATECH was to solve common manufacturing problems and regain US competitiveness over Japan. Today, its members represent about half of the worldwide chip market. When government strategically engages with the private sector, we can accomplish great things, and SEMATECH is a brilliant example.

How do we start? How about we convene? This is how government draws focus. It will pick a topic and convene thought leaders, business leaders, and the right mix of people from government to think through some of these challenges and come up with some standards. We have a very difficult time advocating for solutions when there are no standards for comparison.

Also, streamlining some of the regulatory challenges that entrepreneurs face is a huge need that government could fulfill without spending any money. "The valley of death" that some entrepreneurs face while they deal with various regulatory hurdles as they try to launch their companies is staggering. It could easily be addressed if the key market makers, entrepreneurs, and government leaders meet with a mindset that they are going to make a positive difference in unlocking the regulatory hurdles that face climate wealth.

What next? Create a plan or a roadmap. People like to be able to see and articulate shorter- and longer-term milestones when it comes to large initiatives such as these. What is success in five years? Ten? We need benchmarks to chart progress. We need accountability and ownership, and, above all, we need the will to follow through.

There are some obvious examples, I think, that would be easy to look at initially. For one, government can and should make it clear that meeting the renewable portfolio standards and efficiency standards that states have already approved will not destabilize the grid. This myth remains active and is used by many as an argument against progress. Government could create a working group that would focus exclusively on the lowest-cost path to implementation for the states to help move this along. Demonstrating action and accomplishment quickly would go a long way to bolster confidence.

We also see now the vital importance of grid infrastructure resilience in the wake of Sandy and other destructive disasters. The Public Service Commission needs guidelines on how to do this, much as we fortified our data and security systems after 9/11. This is a matter of urgency. In President Obama's inaugural address, he said:

> *We will respond to the threat of climate change, knowing that the failure to do so would betray our children and future generations.*
>
> *Some may still deny the overwhelming judgment of science, but none can avoid the devastating impact of raging fires, and crippling drought, and more powerful storms. The path toward sustainable*

energy sources will be long and sometimes difficult. But America cannot resist this transition. We must lead it.

We cannot cede to other nations the technology that will power new jobs and new industries. We must claim its promise.

Clearly, the US government and the Obama administration see our future for jobs and the economy directly linked to addressing our climate issues. So my point here is that we can turn this rhetoric into a new climate wealth reality.

Another area where attention by government is needed is on our drinking water facilities, which, according to the American Society of Civil Engineers, are in need of $55 billion in investment to bring them up to par. The water authorities have taxing power, so raising this money is not difficult. But implementing next-generation technologies to minimize rate increases is very difficult. There must be a plan or pathway for this gross underinvestment that would help us to implement technologies we ourselves invented.

I also strongly believe that fuel choice should be the other half of the equation. The hegemony of oil over all other transportation fuels must end if we are going to make progress. This is tough for many to swallow, but government must lead on this and come out in word and deed to level this playing field.

How can they do that? I have said it many times, and some are surprised, but I believe we must put an end to confusing subsidies for mature and legacy industries. Large fossil fuel companies continue to corner the market because of strategic subsidies that are not expensive but that shift the dynamics such that others cannot compete. Fossil fuels are not the only ones. There are other mature industries such as solar that benefit now. But if the game were fair and (again back to the notion of standard creation) if consumers could compare their options with equal and fair standards, I believe they would make different choices. Solar does not need subsidies to be successful, as we are seeing, but taking away unfair competition would help in many areas. In other words, may the best solution win on its own merit.

California, Germany, and Japan have shown us how smart legislation and policy can help. New technologies can scale quickly with some government support and then sunset (end) the government provisions after some reasonable period of time. This will eliminate an endless expected government support for an industry. Gasoline for fuel transportation does not need to be subsidized. And if gasoline were ten dollars per gallon, consumers would demand other fuel options for transportation—and the economics would change.

People do understand that new technologies sometimes need a kick-start to get going, but in these austere fiscal times endless support provisions are not palatable, and they are simply not fair. If the new ideas scale correctly in the provided time, they won't need the help. And if they don't, the market will dictate their demise.

Finally, government needs to lead by example here. The federal government is an enormous customer with huge buying power. It should be leading the way as a first mover wherever possible. For example, government buildings, land, and other assets can be used to demonstrate how, and if, these new solutions can be cost-efficient, energy-efficient, and reasonable to implement. The government is one of the largest energy users. It has the ability to create market demand by making some of these choices, showing the way for states and other large consumers as well as for individuals.

Other simple examples include the government's ability to use additional free market tools such as the Super Energy Savings Performance Contacts, power purchase agreements for electricity generation, and other proven structures to unlock the $150 billion in federal government purchases for electricity, mobility, and water.

I have said it before: infrastructure investment is the largest wealth creation opportunity on the planet—and today's opportunity is in climate wealth creation. Globally, the World Bank estimates it to be at least $35 trillion over the next twenty years, and here in the United States it is believed to be more than $2.2 trillion. We cannot leave that on the table. But to really get climate wealth moving, we require leadership from the government. This is not a partisan issue; this is an economic issue. There is room for many perspectives, and in fact we benefit from both sides in the sense that Republicans feel business should be unencumbered, and Democrats feel government has a role. It is, as I said in the *Fast Company* article, not so much a balance of power but rather a balance of control and chaos. We can achieve this balance. We must. And government can lead by example.

CHAPTER SEVEN:

Why Service Companies Have an Edge in the Infrastructure Space

The solutions to infrastructure discussed in earlier chapters carry an upfront cost. It feels more expensive to buy something that is economically efficient because the costs are greater at the beginning, while the savings come over time.

In the case of solar, there are more upfront costs for the equipment, but over time there are no fuel costs. And we get all of our money back—and more. So the challenge becomes getting consumers to make that initial investment.

It's the same story with natural gas. Although more expensive than diesel—natural gas prices are half the price of diesel right now—installing a natural gas engine carries a one-year payback. But the problem is that most people don't want to pay an upfront cost. They don't want to part with $20,000 or more.

Service-based SunEdison, for example, signs customers up for a twenty-year contract and then charges them for power, the same way they'd pay a utility company over time. They pay off the principal plus interest.

In the natural gas industry, for instance, here is how it could work: a salesperson says, "I'm going to sell you a natural gas package, and you pay me what you would have paid for diesel. You pay ten thousand dollars instead of twenty thousand, and then I'll charge you three dollars a gallon for natural gas for the next two years to pay myself back for the natural gas engine."

Cost-Efficient Way of Selling Infrastructure

An entire body of work deals with how one changes infrastructure from a product-based to a service-based offering. There is no better example than solar. Retailers, for example, have found that solar service agreements for commercial and large industrial systems are the only way to go. It's blatantly obvious: why would anyone pay upfront for a solar system and get into the power plant business?

What most people don't understand is that that same thinking can be applied in seventeen different sectors—from industrial efficiency to commercial-building efficiency. For instance, technology can reduce lighting expenses by 65 or 70 percent. The only glitch is that it costs money upfront and takes eighteen months to pay back the upfront premium.

Most people, however, budget year to year and prefer not to spend money on something that they deem "noncore" to the business. Our logical response to customers is: "We'll give it to you, and you pay us back most of the savings you would get using the system. After two or three years, we'll be paid off with interest, and the savings are yours."

The same principle is applicable in agriculture, where an industrial-farming operation can take advantage of drip irrigation rather than flooding fields, paring water consumption by 70 to 80 percent. It's worth it because water is precious. It works the same way. Someone else pays for the drip-irrigation system and then gets paid back out of the water savings.

But those are only a few examples. Several service models are available. The problem is we're used to selling products. If you ask companies such as Honeywell, GE, or Carrier (the air-conditioning manufacturer) why they're having problems selling their high-efficiency units, the companies will say it's because the units cost 50 percent more. And they don't offer financing or service-based agreements.

The problem is their CFOs want to book the profits upfront. Service contracts require you to spread the profits over the life of the service contract. As a result, they sell very few high-margin, high-efficiency units. Almost everyone makes his or her buying decisions based upon upfront cost.

The importance of adopting a service-based model can be understood in terms of the "tipping point" that Malcolm Gladwell identified in his groundbreaking book *The Tipping Point: How Little Things Can Make a Big Difference*. The tipping point "is that magic moment when an idea, trend or social behavior crosses a threshold, tips and spreads like wildfire," Gladwell wrote.

The widespread adoption of a service-based model would change the way people buy things. It is a proven concept that is on the threshold of becoming a significant trend that could change the way many expensive products are sold. We are at this tipping point for solar PV today.

Many of the technologies discussed in this book were invented in the 1970s but never made it to prime time because consumers didn't want to pay for something and then save money over time. For example, very few people will pay an extra 15 percent for their homes knowing they'll save on their heating and air-conditioning bills over the next twenty-five years. They'd rather buy the least-expensive house that meets their needs. The problem is most consumers have been conditioned to think about buying products based upon their upfront costs.

The thinking is pervasive and applicable to most industries: lighting, agriculture, manufacturing, and shipping, to name a few. It's amazing how many technologies make financial sense, but no one wants to install them because of their upfront costs. Changing this mindset will unlock the greatest wealth creation opportunity on the planet.

CHAPTER EIGHT:

Don't Be Fooled by Randomness

"Good luck is another name for tenacity of purpose."
—Ralph Waldo Emerson

A few years after I started SunEdison, I read the most influential book in my life: *Fooled by Randomness: The Hidden Role of Chance in Life and in the Markets*, by Nassim Nicholas Taleb. It is Taleb who makes the case that everyone looks brilliant when things are going well—the economic conditions are right, and trend data support our efforts. But the important question is, "Is success the result of timing or trends or management acumen?" (Taleb, 2001)

For me, SunEdison was filled with serendipity and purposefulness. In 2003, one of my partners insisted we submit our business plan to the Harvard Business School case competition. My response was: "Do it without me; I don't need Ivy League validation." She did, and through it we found our fourth partner, who was very critical to our success. In 2005, President Bush passed the Energy Policy Act of 2005, which increased the tax credit for solar from 10 to 30 percent. This was a huge benefit for us. We had just closed our financing fund with Goldman Sachs in June 2005, and none of us predicted that this could happen. These events weren't something we lobbied or planned for. They just happened to work in our favor.

When opportunity presents itself and we're not prepared for it, it doesn't happen. When it does—even though we are not prepared—to me, that's luck.

Many people mistakenly take credit for events triggered by marketing efforts and hype. If we believe the hype—which can be disarmingly seductive—we're likely to make mistakes that can cause our companies to fail. Entrepreneurs must have long vision and look past what is right in front of them on the horizon as they plan for the changes that are inevitably coming.

Except for lottery winners, there is no such thing as luck per se. Preparation and planning is key.

If the world is eager for a solution that solves an electricity-pricing problem, for example, we have to be ready to pounce on any opportunity that crops up, whether it is favorable legislation or the right economic factors. If we don't have our contracts ready, financing in place, in short, all the essential pieces necessary to take advantage of a favorable trend, we'll miss our chance to capitalize on it. That is not bad luck. That is bad planning.

I firmly believe that we can change the course of our own lives through hard work and perseverance. But things also serendipitously happen for which we don't plan. It's important to recognize what we can control and influence and what we can't control. If we can't make these distinctions, we won't be able to replicate our successes. In other words, when that "luck" does happen, the successful entrepreneur must be able to attribute the success to specific plans and actions so that he or she can ensure that it can happen again. Inflated and distorted egos can blur that critical distinction and lead to disastrous mistakes.

Entrepreneur Jason Cohen, founder of technology companies WP Engine and Smart Bear Software, summed up the impact of luck as follows: "Your best bet for success is to treat all your decisions as empirical tests. Confidence and experimentation are not contradictory. Try anything, measure everything and follow what works, even if that means changing everything. Then you can be lucky, too" (Cohen, 2009).

Explaining entrepreneurial success, Cohen says, "Overall success in business doesn't mean you 'got luck,' it means you used luck, taking advantage of the good, identifying and canceling the bad" (Cohen, 2009).

Luck has never been part of investing guru Warren Buffett's investing philosophy. Two of Buffett's seven secrets for living a happy life are to think simply and to live a simple life. He explains thinking simply this way: "I want to be able to explain my mistakes. This means I do only the things I completely understand" (O'Laughlin, 2003).

And of living a simple life, Buffett says, "I just naturally want to do things that make sense." Those secrets of a simple life carried over to Buffett's investment philosophy, which made him the nation's fourth-wealthiest person, according to *Forbes* magazine in 2013.

Buffett has always avoided investing in Internet stocks, for example, because he doesn't understand how they work. The fact that they've made a lot of people very wealthy is beside the point. That's a level of discipline very few fund managers displayed in the late 1990s.

Impact economy entrepreneurs and investors would do well to follow Buffett's lead.

The impact economy should focus its energy on areas that are making a proven difference and stay clear of areas that are limited to being just award-winning TED presentations. (TED is a nonprofit devoted to "Ideas Worth Spreading" and famously hosts "talks" on topics related to technology, entertainment, and design.) There are many success stories in clean agriculture, clean energy, and clean water. And there are many pilot programs that have been successful as well. It's critically important that we understand why they were successful so we can replicate the successes. This is why this level of understanding is so important in this space—more so than others because the solutions for which we are advocating are life-changing, economy-driving potential solutions to problems that affect millions of people.

Take the fashion industry, for example. Many entrepreneurs were enormously successful because they either capitalized on a trend or created one while others failed miserably. But the entire world isn't negatively affected by the fashion world's successes or failures. Not so in the impact economy, where every success can positively affect the entire world.

In America, our efforts to rid ourselves of our dependence on foreign oil have been foiled by randomness. We've been so fooled by randomness that every time we think there is a trend pointing to a sustained increase in oil prices, oil prices plummet. Every time we think we are going to benefit from cheap oil for the rest of our lives, oil prices soar. Or every time we think we know where all the hot spots are in terms of where oil disruption can occur, something unexpected happens. Even the smartest people in the oil industry cannot predict the future.

But the Brazilians just decided that they needed to rid themselves of their oil addiction. They endured ridicule over their ethanol strategy, which today has freed them from oil at a time when oil hovers around one hundred dollars per barrel. Just in time, they also found one of the largest oil finds off their east coast. Was this energy independence twice over luck or planning? In this case, the ethanol was planning; the oil find was a bonus.

Using past events as our guide and teacher, we must figure out how to focus on areas where our efforts are making a difference and de-emphasize areas where luck accounted for success. By definition, entrepreneurs must do these calculations. If they don't, they fail.

Similarly, governments must figure out which policies work and which ones are just taking credit for things that would have happened anyway. This lack of introspection causes governments around the world to waste money trying to support industries at prodigious rates. Entrepreneurs matter and should be supported, but governments must be able to tell the difference between creating a wave and riding a wave. When they don't, money is wasted.

As Taleb wrote in *Fooled by Randomness*, "Reality is far more vicious than Russian roulette...it delivers the fatal bullet rather infrequently, like a revolver that would have hundreds, even thousands of chambers instead of six. After a few dozen tries, one forgets about the existence of a bullet, under a numbing false sense of security" (Taleb, 2001). That's sound advice impact economy entrepreneurs and investors ought to heed.

CHAPTER NINE

Market Timing Is Everything

"There is one thing more powerful than all the armies of the world, and that is an idea whose time has come."
—Victor Hugo

Regardless of industry, no one can question the power and influence of market timing. When selling infrastructure as a service, the critical questions for entrepreneurs and government decision-makers are: How do we look at market timing? How should we evaluate it? And how do we strategically use it to our best advantage?

There are two forces at work that positively affect market timing: the first force, technology, is getting cheaper; the second force, technology improvements—newer and cooler apps—are getting more expensive.

In the 1990s, California tried to mandate electric vehicles. The California Air Resources Board said that by 1998, 2 percent of all new cars sold in the state must have "zero tailpipe emissions." The mandate called for an increase to 5 percent by 2001 and 10 percent by 2003.

When Bill Clinton was elected president in 1992, oil soared from fifteen dollars a barrel to thirty. By 1998, the price dropped back to fifteen. With gas at one dollar to $1.20 a gallon, electric vehicles weren't the first thing on people's minds.

Unfortunately, California Gov. Jerry Brown's eco-visions never came to fruition because the market timing was all wrong. No matter how badly

Californians wanted the mandate, the major carmakers wouldn't have it. Sound concept, bad timing.

More recently, oil prices rose to $147 a barrel and then dropped to $110, sliding further to eighty-five. Now consumers believe oil prices will be volatile and high in the future, which wasn't true in the past.

Market Timing Is Everything

In the unpredictable world of products and services, whether consumer or business-to-business, there's no divine law that says the best products always conquer the marketplace. The history of technology is littered with breakthrough products—hardware, software, and services—that bombed in the marketplace. And some less-than-mediocre products were runaway best sellers.

Those realities underscore the importance of heeding and respecting the mysterious laws of market timing.

No matter how much money you put into a product—designing, manufacturing, and promoting—if you're way ahead of the market, you've wasted time and money. All you've accomplished is that you've given product reviewers something to write about and first adopters something to add to their collection of defunct products no one will remember.

Market Timing and Infrastructure

The rules of market timing are especially important in infrastructure. There is no way someone will give you a trillion dollars unless the technology you're selling has proven itself, and that usually means the technology has been out a minimum of twenty years before it's ready to take off and scale. History has proven this repeatedly, and it's also taught us that the best product doesn't always win.

We can't forget that the technologies that were around in the early 1990s were too expensive to remotely control. Now they can be remotely controlled because mobile devices have become more sophisticated and affordable. It's certainly a lot cheaper than installing more landlines or upgrading ones installed decades ago.

By the same token, technology never surprises us in the infrastructure space. What surprises us are breakthroughs in deployment models, which depend upon stakeholders' being excited enough about the technology to make infrastructure a top priority. That's critically important because the challenges we're talking about are not easy to overcome.

There are many straightforward approaches to the adoption of solar, but the right conditions have to be in place to make it happen. For example, after enduring a five-day power outage following a hurricane, we can approach a local town council and make a powerful case for passing a law that mandates solar or backup power. That's an optimal moment to introduce smart, viable, and affordable solutions. The problem has caught the attention of politicians who have to respond because their constituents are upset. The situation dictates immediate action. Predictably, politicians are likely to favorably respond to what we're offering. It won't take them long to conclude that we're offering great solutions and pass legislation to make them happen.

But prior to Hurricane Sandy and the subsequent power outage, no one was clamoring for solar because there were dozens of priorities demanding attention. Buildings are crumbling, roads are buckling, and bridges and tunnels are in desperate need of repair, for example. This is why market timing is so important.

Entrepreneurs Don't Get It

Entrepreneurs don't understand the rules and realities of market timing. All they know is that people aren't listening to them. They don't understand why no one is even trying to get their hands around their big ideas. They see proven solutions that are being ignored. The reality is that government has other things it deems more important.

It drives home the point made earlier. People pay attention to finding solutions to immediate problems. It can be likened to a doctor saying to a patient, "You look very healthy, but if you don't take these medications every day, your health will be in jeopardy in the future."

The patient thinks, the doctor is talking about the future, two to five years down the road. I feel fine now, so why deal with the problem now?

People buy pain medications when they're in acute pain. So we want to make sure that people are in acute pain and demand pain medications, so to speak. In other words, they must feel that the solution is necessary. Apply that analogy to infrastructure, and we see immediate results. Give people solutions that look like pain medications, and they'll be eager to implement them.

Again, it all comes down to market timing.

This is why entrepreneurs in the infrastructure space don't live in a vacuum. It's because what people in government and others believe actually matters. Plus, infrastructure usually has a high barrier to entry and requires permits and regulations from the government.

In other areas, technology reigns supreme. What better example is there than social networking? The infrastructure of the Internet was already in place. Scaling social networking did not require government intervention. It quickly became so popular that it didn't matter what was going on in other sectors or in government. But that's not the case with infrastructure.

At the moment, agriculture is a key concern because people are worried about dwindling food supplies and the effects of global warming upon growing seasons. Solutions to the pressing problems are needed right now. The market is screaming for solutions. A decade ago, no one cared about agriculture, so politicians turned a deaf ear.

Five years ago, everyone had concerns about the water supply. But there was no apparent emergency. Even though data confirmed we had a water crisis, the politicians weren't ready to apply pressure because their constituents weren't complaining. Again, it's further reinforcement that market timing matters.

Too often, passion takes over, hurling facts and reason to the sidelines. Entrepreneurs have what they think are irrefutable solutions to pressing problems. And they have customers willing to support and buy the solutions. They think they have everything needed to lay the groundwork for success. With all the variables in place, they don't understand why they can't get backing.

The answer is disarmingly simple. The market isn't ready for the solutions, even though logic, principles, and data irrefutably support their assertions.

They don't understand the mysterious workings of market timing, which must be respected. It's a hard truth for entrepreneurs who have poured their hearts and souls into something they believe in, not to mention put themselves in hock for.

Entrepreneurs in the impact space potentially have seventeen different sectors with which to work. I will be exploring several of them in detail in later chapters of this book. The important point is that each one has its own rhythm, which forces entrepreneurs to strategically time their solutions so that they make maximum impact.

I'm not saying it's easy knowing when the timing is right. But one thing is certain: in order to create the impact economy, market timing not only matters, but it also requires serious thought, study, and understanding.

Take electricity rates, for example, which have recently jumped. Consumers have had to deal with sudden, unpredictable weather changes and often-lengthy power outages. Meanwhile, utility companies keep on increasing their rates. Consumers are ready to switch to solar. It is why we are starting to see increased adoption of solar in the residential market. Remember, SunEdison really started by focusing on commercial buildings like Wal-Mart, Staples and Whole Foods stores.

But in the transportation sector, it's a different story. People aren't saying, "What's wrong with my car? I'm ready for an alternative." Gasoline prices have dropped, and electric cars are getting better, but they're far from affordable for the average consumer. Meanwhile, the car companies are trying to figure out how to make electric cars more affordable.

Markets exist only when there are customers, and there are predictable buying patterns. Until there is a proven market, it's hard to get funding, even from venture capitalists who are used to dealing with nascent demand.

When we're way ahead of the market, there are always early adopters to whom to sell. But they're hardly a reliable indicator of future demand. And customers seldom know what they need or how much they're willing to pay for something. It's up to entrepreneurs to have a crystal-clear vision and be willing to tweak their products several times until the market is ready to buy them.

CHAPTER TEN:

Never Underestimate the Value of a Business Card and a Potential Relationship

Every year, billions of business cards are passed out. I'd guess that every second of the day someone on the planet is handing someone—client, customer, contact—his or her business card.

Even with today's multibillion-dollar social networking industry, networking is still a face-to-face encounter. Every year, millions of people hand out their business cards at networking events, hoping that a few will be the door-opener for some kind of business relationship. It is a numbers game, plain and simple. The more business cards you hand out, the better the odds of achieving your goal.

Even though social networking has changed the way we network, the business card, like appropriate business attire and résumés, will always be a ubiquitous prop on the global business stage. Whether bookkeeper or CEO, the vast majority of us leave home with a neat little stack in our pockets. The business card goes part and parcel with getting ahead, career building, and success.

I discovered the power of the business card in my early twenties. Although I'm always meeting new people at conferences, symposia, and business events, I've never been an aggressive networker. Yet I've always liked meeting people. Over the years, I have come to understand how important those connections and impressions can be. Treating people respectfully is of the highest importance.

Karma and Connections

For me, I don't meet people just to do business with them as much as I simply think sharing is about karma – give and ye shall receive. According to Buddhist thinking, karma is the belief that whatever we do comes back to us. Simply, if you do something good, something good will happen to you and vice versa. In most Indian religions (Hinduism, Buddhism, Sikhism), karma is about cause and effect. Certain laws decide what effect results from a given cause. Karma describes the cause part. Our actions create our karma.

In the business world especially, we need supporters rooting for our success.

By the same token, there are a lot of people who are mean and nasty, and it's reflected in the way they do business. Their motives are less than honorable; their goal is to squeeze every nickel out of a business deal. The result is everyone comes away from business transactions feeling a little dirty.

Unscrupulous and underhanded people are as much a part of the business landscape as the honest people working hard to get ahead. Like predators in the wild, they're part of the business environment, and they are not going away. Their very existence emphasizes the importance of being nice.

When I look back on SunEdison's early years, I'm awed and amazed by the positive impact people have had on us. From the onset, everyone in the solar industry wanted us to be successful. This is something that I couldn't have planned. We didn't solicit support in our mission statement or website. It just happened.

Everyone we worked with—employees, customers, banks, and the finance community—believed in what we were doing. College students who read about us wanted us to succeed. Even now, I get letters from people I met in those early years.

The Eye-Opener

The powerful lesson is that good things happen when we're nice to people and when other people are nice to us. This is why a business card matters.

While the business card indicates our status or position or the businesses we work for or own, on another level it's a convenient piece of paper. It transcends impressive titles and high-value prefixes in front of our names.

When we give people our business card, we're making a statement of good intent. We're telling them that we think they're important in some way. Maybe we want to work with them, buy from them, hire them, learn from them—or possibly there is no motive at all. It could be as vague as a gut feeling that they're nice people worth knowing.

Unlike the consumer space, where transactions are straightforward and brief, in the infrastructure sector, business transactions are complex, and the buyer/seller relationship is ongoing. The exchange of a business card in the infrastructure space can mark the beginning of a long and involved professional relationship.

It's difficult enough constructing a solar project, but once it is up and running, it has to operate successfully without glitches for twenty years. Our ability to get more work is predicated on how well every system we sell performs. It also depends on the real relationships we build with the people and the communities we serve with the life-changing solutions we offer.

This is why the business card is so important. Practically every person we meet could be essential to our success.

When I was in my mid twenties and someone I thought highly of, whether in the solar industry or finance community, gave me his or her business card, I was very flattered and felt I was on top of the world. Not everyone we meet has that kind of impact. We may meet and shake hands with the mayor of our city. He'll pat us on the back and say, "Don't forget to vote for me in November," but he's not going to give us his business card.

It's to everyone's advantage to see the business card as a symbolic gesture of respect and sincere interest. It's very easy to lose sight of this when things are going our way. If our business suddenly takes off, we shouldn't let success go to our heads and stop sharing our business cards with people who impress us in some way, whether we plan to do business with them or not. It's impossible to predict what happens to all the people who pass through our business and personal lives. They could be brilliant people from whom we learn a great deal, or they may be nice people we may consider hiring in two or three years.

Respecting the value of a business card and the importance of treating everyone we meet with respect creates a favorable impression that people don't forget.

As I said earlier, we at SunEdison discovered that a number of things went our way because people were looking out for us. We discovered that the State of California had an open request for proposal (RFP) for a system similar to our business model. A conversation with a principal at research-and-advisory firm Clean Edge (www.cleanedge.com) led to inclusion as one of the "Select Organizations to Watch" in their "Clean Energy Trends 2012, March Report."

In the course of doing business, just being nice to people—helping them out, providing advice or references to capable people we knew—came back to us a hundred-fold. We left people with a good impression of us. People who didn't know us but heard or read good things about us led to a very favorable industry-wide impression. People thought we were genuine, the real deal.

And that's how contacts were made and contracts won. It's happened over and over again. And it all started because I was nice to someone for five minutes. She told others, and the word spread. It's not only the right way to do business, but it also goes part and parcel with relating and connecting to people in a meaningful, constructive way. Because we went out of our way to have good experiences with everyone, people were more inclined to help us.

But not everyone subscribes to that simple philosophy. Some people make snap mental calculations about people based upon their perceived value. "That guy isn't important. He doesn't get a business card."

Not true. One day that person we summarily dismissed as irrelevant is suddenly important because we need him or her to intervene on our behalf. It harkens back to the importance of treating everyone the same way. It's unproductive to box people into categories or put them on lists based upon their presumed value. It's not only way too complex and unnecessary, but we are also judging people—valuing some, devaluating others. That doesn't mean there is zero differentiation, but it does mean we ought to try to respect and treat everyone the same way.

It's all about the power and importance of personal interactions and how we can positively influence everyone we meet and with whom we deal. It comes down to personal choice. For me, it was simple, uncomplicated, and yet incalculably rewarding in the end.

CHAPTER ELEVEN

Know Your Customers and Keep Them Happy

Whether we're selling to consumers or businesses, the phrase, "The customer is always right," coined by London entrepreneur Harry Gordon Selfridge (founder of Selfridges department store in 1909), has ascended to a commandment successful entrepreneurs respect and by which they live. It doesn't matter whether we're selling toothbrushes or diesel trucks, bicycles or solar power systems; the simple credo underscores the importance of listening to customers and understanding and meeting their needs. It applies universally to all industries, products, and services.

As important as the customer/seller relationship is, in infrastructure it's ultimately more important than it is in the consumer space. Most consumer transactions are transitory and forgotten moments or days after they're consummated.

In infrastructure, the business relationships are far more complicated because our typical customer is never a single person.

Even when we're installing a solar energy system in someone's home, several residents have a say as well as the local government. And at the corporate level, the business relationship extends far beyond the actual buyer and seller. For instance, we may be initially working with the energy manager, who's very enthusiastic about solar. But he reports to the operations manager, who is not only in charge of energy but is also responsible for operating the business for the next twenty years. And he in turn reports to and works closely with the CFO, who is concerned about making sure the balance sheet looks good because it's a publicly traded company; he has to be obsessively diligent about meeting quarterly targets.

But it doesn't end there. The CEO and chief marketing officer have a new initiative to save costs and buy "green" all to enhance their brand. But the proverbial buck doesn't stop even there; wait until legal and investor relations get involved.

The Complexities of the Business Stage

The business relationship always starts with a conversation with one person, the energy manager, for example. From that point on, as the relationship evolves, more people enter and exit the business stage, and each one's role is important.

Most importantly, we have to work with all of them. We must answer their questions, meet their requirements, and go out of our way to give them whatever they need to be satisfied with our service.

The reason there are so many people in the business equation is because infrastructure is something that is going to last for a long time. For that reason alone, one person doesn't make all the decisions. The organization makes the decision. There are significant regulatory limitations, too, because for the most part these solutions and decisions are fairly irreversible.

If one person does make all the decisions, it's likely an experimental pilot program. A large company searching for an energy-efficient solution may test a solar installation at one store in order to gauge its value, for example. If the pilot program is successful, we can't assume that we're a shoo-in for winning contracts for the next two hundred locations. We have to go back to square one and satisfy all the players in the potential relationship.

Don't Fall into the Technology Trap

Whether investor or entrepreneur, we must avoid the technology trap by thinking our technology matters to the customer. It's a mistake to focus our sales pitch on the technology's benefits, such as efficiency, aesthetics, and chemistry. All too frequently, the result of such myopic thinking is drawing false conclusions, such as, "If management doesn't buy our technology, they're idiots."

Many smart entrepreneurs fall into this trap and fail to see how their work fits into the bigger picture. Unquestionably, state-of-the-art technology is important, but in infrastructure customers only want the end service—electricity, clean water, and mobility. More important is understanding all the friction points of our customers and then making an irrefutable case that meets the needs of the organization, from CEO to the energy managers and technicians.

On another level, we have to educate and update our colleagues so that they not only support our efforts but also understand all the nuances of the system, such as how to maintain the infrastructure, anticipate and troubleshoot problems before they occur, and what to do if something goes wrong. What crisis management and backup strategies are in place to expeditiously solve the problem so service isn't disrupted?

What if dual infrastructure has to be maintained? Companies sell dual-fuel technologies for heavy trucks. Because trucks burn natural gas and diesel fuel, customers could apparently take advantage of the equivalent of a discount on fuel because they're paying, say, four dollars a gallon for diesel but only two dollars a gallon for natural gas. It sounds like a no-brainer. But if the seller doesn't know where the natural gas refueling stations are for the customer's routes, the seller has a serious problem. Potential customers also want to be sure that the maintenance costs for both fuels won't erase the savings.

What initially appears basic, logical, and good business sense often can't be implemented because all the variables and unforeseen problems were not considered. More often than not, this is because entrepreneurs are consumed by their own technology and are not paying enough attention to all the other factors in the customer's view that have an impact on the solution.

Questions surrounding selling are often very basic: What motivated a customer to buy something? What triggered the sale? What problems were solved? But the answers aren't always apparent, and the key players may have different answers.

In sum, many levels of understanding have to be considered so infrastructure can be properly sold, implemented, and maintained.

Lesson Learned about SunEdison Customers

Early on, we realized that SunEdison's customers didn't seem to care about saving money. Initially, we pitched them on saving money, but they didn't seem to care whether they saved one dollar or $10,000. Most of our customers' stores had more than $5 million in annual sales; $10,000 just didn't mean that much. What mattered to them was locking in their rate for twenty years because they were fed up with all the volatility in their budgets.

CFOs had to endure the ulcer-generating uncertainty of constantly adjusting to fluctuating electricity rates. If electricity rates climbed by 7 percent, they would have to figure out where to cut costs to make their budgets work. They simply wanted predictable pricing, the certainty of knowing what their energy costs would be next year and the year after that. That continuity of pricing, which we were able to offer, was what they valued the most.

I would venture to say that most of the solar PV industry still sells on savings instead of price predictability. This underscores the importance of asking our customers questions—very basic questions—at the outset in order to find out what's important to them, particularly to identify their most important problems.

By asking these very basic questions, entrepreneurs gather essential information about their customers. They avoid guessing or making assumptions. They may discover that their customers buy for different reasons. Some may buy to brag about their green credentials, others for consistent pricing, others because our product is best suited for specific needs. If we don't understand what those needs are, we're winging it, and the futures of our companies are in jeopardy.

CHAPTER TWELVE:

Work with the Best. Hire the Best.

Choosing the best people is more complicated than most people realize. It's not as simple as interviewing five or six people and picking one we think is the best of the lot. Hiring the right people is one of the most important decisions entrepreneurs face.

How do we determine who is the best? What are the criteria for making that decision? Most entrepreneurs don't take the time to answer these questions. They take the easy path and too often suffer the consequences later.

There is a prevailing notion, for example, that passion alone can make up for fundamentals. The thinking has become so popular that many companies have elevated it to one of the single most important attributes for evaluating potential hires—especially in terms of impact.

Expectedly, job-hungry candidates pick up the passion ball and run with it, intertwining passion and skills when selling themselves on their résumés and in interviews.

Let's Get Real

Don't get me wrong. I'm not discounting the importance of passion; it is critical to success. However, passion can't supersede being the best in your field. Whether it's finance, sales and marketing, or technology, certain skills and traits identify the most qualified people in each niche.

Speaker, author, and coach Curt Rosengren has said, "You can dream all you like, but a career you love happens in the real world. And except for the occasional stroke of blind luck, success in the real world doesn't come by waving a magic wand. It comes from trusty standbys like hard work, ability and persistence" (Rosengren, 2008).

And "passion won't miraculously make it happen," Rosengren said, "but it *can* play an important role. It can give you energy to put into creating success. It can give you a sense of confidence. And it can feed the persistence you need to succeed. But the success itself? You'll have to do that the old-fashioned way" (Rosengren, 2008).

Many companies have paid a hefty price for not respecting the complexities of the hiring process, one of which is identifying the criteria determining the most-qualified candidates. I remember learning early on that you had to dedicate real resources to HR and make that function part of your inner circle.

Organizations Learn the Hard Way

A recent CareerBuilder survey concluded that bad hires lower companies' productivity, affect worker morale, and often result in legal issues.

Here are the survey's findings:

> ➤ Forty-one percent of companies estimate that a bad hire costs more than $25,000 in direct expenses, plus more than $50,000 in lost worker productivity and for recruiting and training new workers.
> ➤ Every bad hire has a negative effect on employee morale.
> ➤ When survey participants were asked why they made bad hiring decisions, 34 percent said they couldn't provide a concrete reason. When pressed, "rushed decisions" topped the list for choosing the wrong candidates.
> ➤ Additionally, 21 percent said "insufficient talent intelligence" contributed to bad hiring decisions. Translated, hirers failed to carefully scrutinize job candidates. And 11 percent failed to perform reference checks.

Defining a Bad Hire

The CareerBuilder survey identified the following six characteristics of a bad hire:

1. Failure to produce quality work
2. Failure to work well with other employees
3. Negative attitude
4. Attendance problems
5. Customer complaints
6. Failure to meet deadlines

This is why a growing number of competitive organizations go to great lengths to identify the criteria that define excellence. At the Carbon War Room, we used the Predictive Index, or PI, which is a mini-version of the popular Myers-Briggs test, to identify people who were the right fit. "Right fit" is an umbrella term for determining whether they have the right skills and personality traits to "fit" in your company and its culture. The PI told us whether a potential hire has the behaviors and personality traits needed for optimal job performance. Like Michael Jordan's Chicago Bulls, you need a balanced group of people to achieve a high-performing team. One superstar doesn't work.

Some people, for example, are not detail-oriented, yet they want to be a CFO. CFOs are supposed to be conservative, be fascinated with details, have exceptional technical and operational skills, and be able to spot problems that escape the attention of others.

Most importantly, the PI helped us identify highly motivated people who would put their hearts and souls into the fields that best cater to their natural strengths. They're motivated to do their best because they care, and they're good at it.

Happiness indexes and studies indicate that people are not happier if they are paid more. They are happier if they do what they love. The flip side of that is that you don't get access to better talent if you pay more; you just get access to talent that wants more money.

Scottish-American industrialist and philanthropist Andrew Carnegie said, "If you want to be happy, set a goal that commands your thoughts, liberates your energy and inspires your hopes." The best motivation for employees is to surround them with good people, position them for success, and give them a mission that they are proud to accomplish.

The Impact Economy Needs the Best People

The best people are vital to creating an impact economy; in fact, it is the only way we are going to get there. The best people are drawn to positions where they can do the most good. If job candidates see a company that is making a difference and has energy—momentum that is felt as soon as they walk into its offices—they will want to work there. Mix in a good management team that knows the fundamentals of capitalism and leadership, and you have a real winning combination. Such a company attracts people who want to help it achieve its goals and mission. It's important to recognize that achieving the company's goals ought to be the primary motivator for attracting the best people. Once you veer away from that and motivate people with money, there is no going back. You can't motivate them with more perks, impressive titles, and more responsibility. Their immediate reaction will be, "You're running short of cash."

It's critical for impact entrepreneurs to remain focused and never to lose sight of the company's mission, so they're always motivating their people with their core values and helping their people grow into positions they love and that provide a feeling of personal fulfillment.

Once companies get to a point where they're making a lot of money, and they start motivating people with money, the good people always leave. They'll jump ship as soon as they find a better dream.

But employees who are working at jobs where they feel important and valued are going to stay; they're also going to excel at whatever they do. If the company experiences a rough patch, they're not going to bail. They're going to fight for the company and work harder. They're likely to say, "Let's figure out how to fix the problem."

This precedent must be set at the very beginning. You can't switch midstream from being a money-centric organization to being a value-centric organization.

When I was CEO of SunEdison, turnover was ridiculously low because it was a great place to work. I would often ask smart people who worked for other companies to work for us. It would take them less than five minutes to make a decision. Their response: "I've heard wonderful things about the SunEdison's culture. You're not going to pay me much more, but there are other things that are more important."

Guy Kawasaki, author and managing director of venture-capital firm Garage Technology Ventures, has said that companies who set out to make a positive change are the companies that will ultimately be the most successful.

Kawasaki went on to say that the essence of entrepreneurship is about making meaning. "Many people start companies to make money, the quick flip, the dot-com phenomenon," he said. "And I have noticed in both the companies that I've started and funded and been associated with—fundamentally founded to change the world, to make the world a better place, to make meaning—are the companies that make a difference. They are the companies to succeed. My naïve and romantic belief is that if you make meaning, you will probably make money" (Kawasaki, 2007).

Quality-of-Life Issues Are Important

One of the things that our employees and potential hires loved was that we were in the Washington, DC, area. We were the only large, successful, clean tech company from Philadelphia to Richmond. If you were smart and wanted to make a difference, you worked for SunEdison. The shareholders also loved it because whereas California is a beautiful state, in Washington, DC, our employees were paid according to the federal government schedule and could buy a house for $400,000.

Smart People Like Working with People Like Themselves

Along with hiring people who share the company's vision and values and who are very good at what they do, we also discovered that people like working with other smart people. They like being around people like themselves, who really care about what they're doing. People always say that you are only as strong as your weakest link. This is true, and for high-performing teams, this is also painfully obvious—emphasis on the pain.

As hard as we tried to hire the best people, we also had to fire people who didn't fit. Morale is negatively affected when employees start whispering to each other about other workers and ask, "Why was he or she hired?" At SunEdison, we were too busy changing the world to have low-performing teams. We had to pay attention to morale and how our employees felt about their jobs and the people with whom they worked.

We were always committed to giving people the training and mentorship they needed to bring them up to speed and provide feedback so they could do a better job. But if they didn't fit after working for us a year, we let them go. It's an unpleasant task, but it's important to quickly correct hiring mistakes so that the culture of the company is preserved. Even though firing workers is unpleasant, a cornerstone to success is to build a strong work force where everyone carries his or her weight and shares the same values. I never understood why so many companies, particularly in the impact economy, hold on to people who are a poor fit. The result is tension in the ranks because underperforming workers throw off the work rhythms of the other workers. That underscores the importance of letting people go, when necessary, in an expeditious fashion.

Even more important in fast-growing companies is changing fit. When a company is composed of just five people, there are different skills required than when a company has fifty people. In every company, without exception, there are early employees who simply love being generalists and who cannot or will not specialize. These cases are the most problematic because early in the company's history everyone needed to do everything. Later in a company's maturity, employees who don't know their boundaries hurt team performance and can cause chaos and mayhem. These cases are especially painful because you know that the employee was critical for the company to get to where it is today. But even in these cases, everyone has to be treated the same. If the employee can't adjust to the new paradigm after receiving intensive training and mentoring then she or he has to be let go for the good of the company.

HR Is King

All of this is to say that a strong human resources (HR) department is important. How do you create a culture that prizes strong values and a powerful, highly motivated work ethic? It's by realizing the importance of HR and believing that it's an important, executive-level, inner-circle position. The head of HR has to be in the inner circle. If he or she isn't, the organization is seriously flawed. Picking an HR director is not only an essential hire; it should also be done early, even if that means stretching the budget. Most companies I know outsource this task to keep costs low, thinking that this is an area they can skimp on until the company is profitable. That's a mistake that always backfires because it means that no one is 100 percent focused on the team and good people. Setting up the culture has to start from day one, or it places the trajectory of the organization's work force in jeopardy.

CHAPTER THIRTEEN

Finding Balance in the Value Chain

Simply put, to build out the $10-trillion opportunity that I've been talking about, everyone has to make money. To consistently deploy roads, bridges, clean water, and energy (solar and electricity), all of the firms throughout the value chain have to be able to make a decent living. Ten trillion dollars is just too much money not to make sure that the benefits are spread around fairly, and this infrastructure affects people's daily lives because everyone depends upon infrastructure. These infrastructure problems are problems that cannot be ignored. If not dealt with in a meaningful and significant way, they will get bigger and create new and more expensive problems.

Here is what I mean: in 2003, the silicon industry was on its back, forced to sell silicon for less than the cost to make it: twenty dollars per kilogram. Because of that, many silicon manufacturers went bankrupt. By 2005, solar was booming, and because the silicon folks couldn't invest in new facilities, the solar industry was short the silicon we needed, and the prices starting going up rapidly. By 2007, silicon topped $200 per kilogram for small quantities, and solar installers were forced to cut their margins to live within the constraints of the rebate program. By 2009, we were in a financial crisis, but the solar installers were so decimated by low margins in 2007–2008 that they were not able to invest the money necessary to significantly expand their sales forces. After keeping all of the profits in 2009, solar installers finally invested in 2010 to put many of the excess panels to work. In just ten years, the solar industry has been in a tug of war of historic proportions, with each part of the value chain failing to respect the other because they felt that they were not respected when the shoe was on the other foot. As a consequence, silicon manufacturers are down again, solar panel manufacturers are no longer viable businesses, and the solar downstream is ignored by many because most have simply dismissed the whole solar industry.

Making sure that people are trained and a basic amount of profit is afforded to all parts of the value chain is essential so that we can meet our infrastructure needs in a way that makes some sense to investors. Because there is so much money floating around in infrastructure, we sometimes attract folks who are unable to see the big picture and are simply focused on maximizing their own firm's profits—to the detriment of the industry at large. If one group takes more than its fair share of profit from the value chain, it either has to come out of someone else's pocket or it results in higher prices to consumers.

This is a critical time. All it takes is one bad experience with the solutions we're talking about—solar power, urban agriculture, clean water, and green lawn-care solutions, for example—and consumers start painting the entire industry as unprofitable and not worthy of investment. Players who are just a bit too greedy have tainted sound solutions.

Greedy business practitioners are not necessarily doing things that are illegal. They are just unnecessarily disruptive and ultimately cause a premature end to the excitement surrounding our solutions because they are shortsighted. Good actors in the marketplace have to complete a lot of steps, and making money while doing things the right way is hard on any given day. They go out into the marketplace and get a lot of people excited about installing solar systems on their roofs or clean-water systems in their basements. But when it comes time to make a final bid price, oftentimes people who are pricing their product at a point that is simply unprofitable undercut them.

Normally, inconsiderate players will go out of business over time. However, for areas like infrastructure, it is a crowded field, and there are often so many players that you could wait years before all the bad actors go out of business.

There is a balance between how much money we get paid, how much money investors get paid, how much lawyers get paid, and how much the maintenance guys get paid to show up and maintain infrastructure assets for the next twenty years. If the greedy players burn one of the parties around the table or take more than their fair share, it creates an unsustainable situation.

Problems are further compounded because there are always distracting success stories. Take the volatile real estate sector, for example. We've all met people who have said: "You're not going to believe this, but I got this great deal on a piece of real estate. I took the seller to the cleaners!" These tall tales or once-in-a-lifetime deals cannot be replicated at a trillion-dollar scale.

What's needed is a regulatory or "best practices" process that allows people to make honest money so that everyone feels good about transactions. In the real estate sector, both buyers and sellers are protected. The people who buy real estate feel good, and the people who sell it feel good. The challenge for people working in this space is what to do about the greedy player.

It's not easy to solve. In most cases people so desperately want to be part of a job that they take a pay cut to stay busy. We all know that we should be paid fairly for our time, but sometimes life just isn't that easy. Variations of this type of scenario play out every day across the nation, underscoring the importance of separating the greedy players from the people trying to create a sustainable industry. If we can't spot the greedy players and pull them off the playing field, the game is corrupted and tarnished, and we're not profit-maximizing our most important asset, which is our time.

The reality is the world is filled with greed—and it's not going away. Like weeds infiltrating throughout a vegetable or flower garden, as soon as they're yanked from the ground, new weeds replace them. In the business world, if they're not dealt with, people start souring on business transactions in general.

Take real estate agents. Whether buying or selling property, most people don't think twice about using them. We're not happy about paying 6-percent fees, yet we keep on relying upon them. Why? Because we believe we're creating a more predictable process and thus better outcomes. We could negotiate real estate deals ourselves, but we believe we're better off having an experienced professional act on our behalf because we believe we'll get a better deal. Unfortunately, we often can't separate the hucksters from the straight players. We often don't know we've been dealt a bad hand until it is too late. In the real estate business, there will always be hucksters who aren't licensed agents and who will negotiate deals for 1-percent fees. But in the end, we get what we pay for.

One of government's roles is to put in place best practice standards. For example, this is what they have done in real estate and auto sales by setting up strict licensing and certification requirements.

The infrastructure space has its own special problems and complexities that need to be addressed. Even though the solar industry is roughly a $90-billion business worldwide, there are few certification requirements. The only reason we have survived so far is because we have so much passion for our work. But passion doesn't pay the bills, so while I continue to be passionate, I am also smart. Finding ways to self-police, monitor, and regulate the infrastructure space is an urgent necessity. Appropriate government intervention wouldn't be a bad idea, either.

CHAPTER FOURTEEN:

Cash-Starved Businesses
Hold Power Hand

In a 2003 interview, Sun Microsystems's cofounder Scott McNealy said many Internet companies bit the dust because they were overcapitalized and fell victim to rampant, needless overspending. McNealy went on to say he couldn't figure out how their investors thought it was a good idea to spend money on expensive Super Bowl ads and expect to run a profitable business. Scott concluded that companies should start like his did, cash-starved. And, being cash starved helped boost Sun in its early days.

Sean Carton, author of *Dot.Bomb Survival Guide*, said the long list of dot-bombers died speedy deaths for many reasons, which include bad business models, failure to identify customers, poorly conceived marketing strategies, and, last but by no means least, overcapitalization. Having too much money often stifles strategic thinking and creative problem solving, which often leads to bad decision making. Overcapitalization also proves that there is often profound truth to the proverb "less is more." Building a business with minimal resources is a powerful teacher. It's real-world learning, which is the only way to disprove disheartening startup statistics (three out of five companies go belly up within three years of launch). But cash-hungry entrepreneurs never get comfortable because every day they face formidable missions: surviving and succeeding.

Emboldened to Succeed

I had already decided to start SunEdison, but the Scott McNealy interview gave me the confidence to think that my small savings might be enough to be successful. I remember thinking to myself, *That's pretty cool. If Scott McNealy can start a cash starved business, so can I.* In the end, the fact that SunEdison was a bootstrapped company that really lived within its means for the first two years opened the door to SunEdison's survival and success.

Like so many other entrepreneurs, I made it work because I had to figure out how to accomplish important tasks without spending money. And I was prepared to do everything possible to achieve my goal.

I figured out a way to use my credit card and not pay interest charges for six months, how to use money creatively, and to stretch every dollar to get maximum value. Most of my first partners took the startup risk with me by not taking a salary for the first eighteen months. But it wasn't easy.

When I approached banks asking for money, they smiled (or laughed) at me. They thought I was either out of my mind or had incredible chutzpah. Their response: "You've got to be kidding. We are not going to give you money unless you've been around for two years." And even then it wasn't going to happen until we turned a profit.

When we finally met an angel investor who agreed to give us money, we wound up rejecting the offer because the partners wanted to hold on to the equity of the company. From January 2003 to December 2004, SunEdison ran off $93,000 from mortgaging my home and $20,000 from my personal savings account and credit cards.

Many successful entrepreneurs learned the importance of being cash-starved rather than overcapitalized. Rather than pay people to solve their problems, entrepreneurs have to learn how to use their ingenuity to solve their problems.

Paul E. Casey, author of *Is Self-Employment for You? Anyone Can Start a Business, Only a Few Can Sustain a Business*, wrote, "Many start-up businesses suffer from the curse of being overcapitalized, rather than undercapitalized. They have too much money in the beginning, rather than too little. The problem with having too much money when you start a business is that you feel obliged to do more, be more, spend more, and grow faster. You feel as if you should maximize your business, make it as big as possible, when in fact you should be keeping your business and its expenditures at an absolute minimum until you establish yourself" (Casey, 2004).

Agreeing with McNealy, Casey said, "The dot-coms were notorious for having too much capital. They spent themselves into oblivion while trying to establish themselves as big names on the Internet frontier" (Casey, 2004).

Casey also said, "You might think that having too much money is the last thing a small-business owner would need to worry about, but I have seen entrepreneurs fail in their ventures for exactly this reason" (Casey, 2004). The reason this is the case is because whereas many entrepreneurs have a good overall concept, the first execution plan is always wrong. If an entrepreneur has a lot of money, he or she pays expensive lawyers and other experts full price to execute the plan. Cash-starved entrepreneurs rarely have enough money to accomplish their first execution plan. While they are raising money, variables change, small parts of the plan are tested, and most importantly things are learned. Even though the entrepreneur has lost six months during the money-raising phase, he or she is also on the fourth version of the execution plan—usually a much better plan.

The Beauty of Toughing It Out

Even today, when I talk to new entrepreneurs, I find that the best ones are the ones who figured out how to make every dollar count. Some describe stories where they had to skip meals or share hotel rooms— I remember those days. Mind you, they made plenty of mistakes and wasted money, which is also par for the course. I certainly made my fair share of mistakes when I started SunEdison.

One of them was giving $20,000 to a consultant in the very beginning because he said he could help me get my company off the ground. He promised the world, so I agreed to everything he said. In the end, he didn't make good on his promises and produced little. I had wasted one-sixth of my startup money.

The experience proved what McNealy drove home in his interview and what Casey repeatedly said throughout his book—companies that are overcapitalized exchange money for future thinking.

If they don't have money, they have no choice but to figure out how to achieve their goals through alternative means because they can't afford to pay someone to take shortcuts.

Priceless Value of Sweat Equity

Throughout SunEdison's startup years, I discovered the meaning of a cash-starved business. Fundamentally, it's very simple. I launched SunEdison with sweat equity rather than other people's money and expertise.

Sweat equity teaches entrepreneurs how to use their core skills, experience, and strategic thinking to make things work. While they're doing it, they learn how to prioritize opportunities to accomplish their goals.

It's especially important for impact entrepreneurs to learn these critical startup survival skills. When they try to solve problems, whether they are with water, health, clean energy, or others, they can't expect anyone to throw a billion dollars at them. If a billion dollars is thrown at a problem—as in through government agencies— the government agencies are probably not going to do it in the way that you think creates the best outcomes. They're likely to do it so that it creates the most political buzz.

Initially, impact entrepreneurs can't wait for people to give them money. They have to figure out how to make things work with what they have at their disposal. That trial-by-fire experience is never forgotten; it's branded in their psyches and attitude and positively affects everything they do. It lays the foundation and paves the road to success.

Even today, I rarely take shortcuts. If there is a problem to solve, I sketch out the solution on my own. There are times when you really need to hire a good law firm, but working the problem first minimizes fees from lawyers. I never say, "Here is two hundred thousand dollars. Why don't you solve this problem for me?" It's not the way I'm wired. Entrepreneurs have to be successful at using strategic thinking to identify problems that can be fixed. I don't need to rely on professional consultants to do it for me.

Just as I learned these business survival skills, it's especially important for impact entrepreneurs to learn problem-solving skills early in the game. It's the only way they'll learn how to leverage and stretch dollars so value is created for shareholders. A cash-starved business, for example, has to create one million dollars of value out of one hundred thousand dollars in the beginning. Achieving that goal attracts professional investors. Venture capitalists want to see that we can generate a tenfold return on their money. If impact entrepreneurs hope to attract a trillion dollars to a solution, they must learn how to create value on that scale. That's the only way they're going to arouse the interest of mainstream investors. In so doing, they'll have to initially balance the amount of impact they are making with the returns they are making.

Attracting the trillion dollars matters. If we want to make more impact, mainstream investors must see real value creation. Otherwise, when your initial funding runs out, so does your impact. There is no shortage of impact investors willing to invest the first $1 million based on a heartbreaking story around building a school, health clinic, or hospital—but finding the next $100 million is difficult with just stories. Real results are what are needed, and the experience derived getting them is invaluable.

If we want mainstream capital sources to give us hundreds of millions of dollars -- or hundreds of billions of dollars, we have to prove to them that we know how to deploy that capital efficiently to achieve adequate risk-adjusted returns. There are dozens of compelling stories of impact entrepreneurs who have mastered the skills necessary to attract the scale of a trillion dollars.

In Africa, three people out of a thousand had access to phones in the late 1990s. Today, close to 70 percent of Africans have phone access. It's because smart entrepreneurs took less than $50 million and created billion-dollar companies. They had to work very hard to get that startup money and multiply it. But they were committed to building successful companies and attracting mainstream investors. They were able to reach their goals with investors who wanted a 35- to 40-percent return on their money.

The result was successful companies that are improving people's lives. Now farmers can use their cell phones to get pricing information about their crops from several vendors so they can get the best price, thus maximizing their profits. Impact investors need these mainstream investors to bring their expertise to the other infrastructure sectors.

A few famous examples are Strive Masiyiwa, Mo Ibrahim, and Denis O'Brien. All three risked politics and safety to bring communications to the masses. In Masiyiwa's case, to start Econet Wireless he fought a landmark constitutional legal battle for five years in Zimbabwe. In Ibrahim's case, he built Celtel across fourteen countries in Africa. As Ibrahim says, "There are too many sub-scale countries in Africa with too many regulations and frontiers; this is a big hindrance. Colonial borders are artificial and cut through ethnic groups and economic activities. What's particularly frustrating is that African governments then go on to apply lots of red tape, which undermines the business environment and regional expansion." O'Brien founded Digicel in 2001, which operates in thirty-one markets with more than 13 million subscribers, as of the end of 2012, in the Caribbean, Central America, and Pacific regions. One of his greatest successes is in Haiti, an unexpected place to find business success over the last ten years.

In 2007, Shai Agassi launched Better Place—a Palo Alto, California-based mobility operator whose goal is to reduce oil dependence by delivering personal transportation as a sustainable service—with $200 million of venture capital. In 2010, he received $350 million in venture capital funding and in 2011 an additional $200 million in venture capital funding. With that level of funding, investors expected impressive results. So Agassi hired expensive professionals, lawyers, and consultants to get results. But, as described above, Shai spent much of the money before really nailing the execution plan. Better Place started with its own technology and took a few years to realize that it was really a mobility services company, which required them to be technology-agnostic. Further, given all the equipment the company was buying, he needed to figure out a way to use non-dilutive project finance to deploy cars. To achieve higher speed, the company spent very expensive equity instead. Agassi is a smart guy, but he threw money at the problem, hoping to solve it. He failed to correctly identify a workable pathway to success. Less money leads to more time working the problem; more money leads to more consultants and more conventional thinking.

Agassi isn't alone. Hundreds of companies have gone belly up because they were overcapitalized. Manu Kumar from K9 Ventures said, "Despite the best intentions, even the most principled founders fall into this trap. They will invariably lose the financial sensibility that they had in their scrappy years." Keeping things lean and mean is important. High-priced consultants are useful for certain projects but not as a replacement for real strategic thinking.

CHAPTER FIFTEEN:
Small Is Beautiful

The twentieth century, in the United States and arguably throughout the world, was defined by the saying "bigger is better." This energizing concept permeated American life—Fortune 500, tree guards for our SUVs in the mall parking lot, McMansions, and over-the-top lifestyles were the hallmarks. For good or bad, big was permanently affixed to everything American.

The term "big business" is a product of the Industrial Revolution, which began following the American Civil War. Smart, aggressive entrepreneurial maverick pioneers, such as John D. Rockefeller, Andrew Carnegie, and J.P. Morgan, consolidated their businesses into massive corporations that grew at unprecedented rates.

The United States far outpaced its competitors by producing products, commercial and consumer, faster and better than other nations. In our quest to be the untouchable leader, big and best were inseparable, practically synonymous components of the success equation. We prided ourselves on creating big businesses, which in turn built factories that turned out big products ranging from ships and cars to bridges, homes, and commercial buildings.

In the United States, BIG is considered the gold standard. Wealth and success are defined by amassing bigger and more expensive things. Big homes, big cars, and big boats are the blatant, in-your-face symbols of wealth. They are inelegant statements that tell the world that a sprawling eight- to fifteen-thousand-square-foot home, outdoor Olympic-size swimming pool, and the Ferrari, Audi, or custom-outfitted Cadillac parked in our driveways are the coveted symbols of wealth.

Politicians intent on building loyal constituencies echoed Americans' quest for big and advocated the virtues of big government because they felt it could meet the needs of Americans. From the military industrial complex to nuclear power, it was big government to the rescue.

Big Government Builds Transportation Infrastructure

It was big government that built our transportation infrastructure—the Transcontinental Railroad in the nineteenth century, the interstate high-way system in the 1950s and '60s, and the national aviation system in the twentieth century. Big government made modern electrification pos-sible in the 1930s and 1940s.

Predictably, institutions embraced the "bigger is better" concept. Large banks, law firms, and investment firms have more clout and power than their smaller counterparts.

Western nations emulated us; developing countries envied us, and the divide between the haves and have-nots widened. Despite America's rapid industrial growth and impressive numbers—especially following the Great Depression—our long-term vision was sullied because we myopically believed that doing things on a large scale was the only way to achieve rapid, sustained growth.

"Big" Defined the American Dream

When law firms and banks looked at investments, they didn't want to consider transactions of less than $100 million. The reasoning was that they could charge big fees and still make the numbers work.

But as the Internet and mobile phone technologies brought project size down, that formula started to fall apart. When applied to clean infrastructure, transaction costs have to be lower. In fact, almost by definition, clean infrastructure has more upfront costs and less operat-ing expenses. This means that loading up the upfront costs make clean infrastructure less cost-effective compared with dirty infrastructure such as coal plants, where construction costs are small compared with the cost of buying coal and maintaining the plant.

With wind energy, for example, the cost of upfront expenditures is far higher, and the ongoing maintenance costs are much lower because there are no fuel costs. It is the same with solar power: free fuel and low maintenance costs. Imagine tacking on an extra 5 or 10 percent on the investment costs; compounding interest costs really can kill a project.

Small Projects Get Done; Large Ones Languish

In addition to transaction costs, large projects have more steps. These steps include needing more money, multiple permits, and government approvals. The result is that the small renewable-energy projects get completed, and larger ones are much harder to push through to the finish. Today, most banks have a limit on how large a transaction can be without calling for help. For big banks, doing a sub-$100-million project is a lot easier than doing one that exceeds $100 million.

For regional banks, loan officers love a $3-million or a $5-million project but get cold feet at numbers above $20 million. Their immediate reaction to small infrastructure projects is: "I like it. I'll invest in it. Let's get the paperwork done."

But it's a different story with billion-dollar projects. Generally, most banks doing large projects have to syndicate above $100 million. That means they have to find ten banks willing to put in $100 million each to complete a billion-dollar project. To put this kind of financing together, they have to engage their investment bankers who always want 2 to 6 percent of the deal.

The upshot is that the most experienced law firms and developers have to figure out how to use technology to make themselves more efficient if they want to succeed in helping to build a more sustainable future. Entrepreneurs are realizing that upfront profits reduce returns, so it is much better to exchange development fees for revenues over time through project ownership. Instead of taking $1 million now, you get $2 million in $200,000-K increments over ten years.

This flexibility is more often found in small companies, not in larger ones subject to quarterly profit targets.

Impact Entrepreneurs Take Matters into Their Own Hands

Resourceful impact entrepreneurs are raising money by themselves; they're doing the engineering, and they are convincing high-priced lawyers to join their firm as in-house counsel—lower salary but better quality of life.

Regardless of the project scope—fuel-saving technologies for heavy trucks, small fertilizer-manufacturing facilities for agriculture, waste-to-energy processes, or septic sewer tanks—most projects are coming in at the sub-$100-million level as opposed to the $100-million-and-up level. In most cases, projects are less than $1 million, making fee management critical to success. These are the projects that the World Bank, the International Finance Corporation, and others should be backing but cannot yet find a way to aggregate up to their minimum investment sizes.

The beauty of doing smaller projects is that because budgets are smaller, and fewer people are involved, there is less chance of corruption. There just isn't enough money in each deal to risk going to jail.

Unquestionably, the "small is beautiful" concept makes sense. But the big question is, "How do we make a trillion-dollar impact at scale by doing small projects?"

The answer: we need to have one million million-dollar projects. Yes, a million times a million is a trillion.

Naysayers' immediate reaction is that it can't be done because it's impossible to get a million million-dollar projects done at scale. And even for solar, newspapers and magazines are enamored with $1-billion projects, not small, insignificant projects. What they don't report is that, in 2011, the solar industry deployed more than $90 billion in projects with an average project size of less than 100 kW—or approximately $400,000 each.

The good news is that we are on track to delivering one million million-dollar solar projects by 2020. The bad news is that mainstream money doesn't yet believe it will happen—or that it matters. The reason is that, of the more than ten thousand solar developers throughout the world, only 10 percent of them are excellent. But the mainstream money folks meet many folks in the 90 percent that don't have the right skills, and it sours them on the entire solar industry.

On a positive note, when we run the numbers, we see that the math still works. If we take a million projects that are $1 million each (a $1-million solar project is 300–500 kW), the thousand good developers have to develop about ten good projects a month over the next eight years. That works out to about $10 million per month, which is an achievable goal. Furthermore, more developers are joining all the time, and while the quality is not consistent the other nine thousand developers will create some projects worth building.

Closing the Great Divide

Today, infrastructure goals are attained by giving contracts to less than one hundred large firms around the world. This is one small part of why we have such a concentration of wealth, the 99 percent versus the 1 percent. The advantage of the "small is beautiful" concept is that small entrepreneurs with low overheads and good tools are doing the development work. Most large companies use law firms and investment firms to do this work. Those firms simply are not set up to do things on a small scale. They can't complete a $1-million project for only $25,000 in fees.

All this underscores the need for small companies to focus on small projects. Many believe that small business is the true engine of growth around the world. By pursuing "small is beautiful" with renewable-energy projects, we're closing the gap between the haves and the have-nots. To make it happen, we have to attract thousands of entrepreneurs content with annual salaries of $250,000 rather than $5 million a year. This is how projects and goals are accomplished expediently and efficiently.

Equally important, $1-million projects aren't scrutinized by government the same way it scrutinizes $50-million projects. The approval process can be likened to building a $1-million house as opposed to a $50-million commercial office building. If all the requirements, permits, licenses, and approval layers are satisfied, building the $1-million house will encounter few or minor obstacles. Count on unforeseen zoning roadblocks delaying the construction of the $50-million building.

But consider the efficacy of building fifty $1-million houses. Not only will we create jobs, but also we will face fewer regulatory hurdles. On the local level, many small projects are exempt from all the rigorous requirements to which big projects are subjected. Another plus is that small entrepreneurs don't have to hire environmental consultants to write impact studies or expensive corporate accountants to do complex calculations determining whether there is a tax infrastructure. More specifically to electricity, small entrepreneurs don't have to submit transmission and distribution studies because smaller projects fit nicely into the existing grid without a lot of necessary changes.

Put all the facts together, and it's not surprising that the average solar project cost in 2011 was less than $400,000. The market is indicating that it is easier to build a $1-million project than it is a $100-million project. And given the low market-entry cost, job creation is faster and dependent only upon the entrepreneur's passion.

Consider the Big-Picture Results

Some 1.3 billion people in emerging markets around the world don't have access to power. For these people, the "small is beautiful" concept is the *only viable way* to change their lives. With high copper prices today, there is no conceivable hope that their governments will connect them to transmission lines. Small community efforts at the $1-million project level is more likely to happen in their lifetime than doing big infrastructure projects.

If we hope to bring sanitation, clean water, clean electricity, and drip irrigation for their farming, it's more likely to happen on a farm-by-farm basis than at the country level.

So whether we are trying to do good in the world or make project sizes more financeable, both goals can be accomplished by adopting the "small is beautiful" strategy.

Section III:
Putting $10 Trillion to Work

Chapter SIXTEEN—

Impact Future: The Carbon War Room

"Climate change is one of the greatest wealth-creating opportunities of our generation."
—Sir Richard Branson, founder of the Carbon War Room

When it comes to questions tapping into the $10-trillion opportunity that I am speaking about, we see once again that "perfect is the enemy of good." Starting sometime in the 1990s, we got hooked on the idea of "technology saving the world," and we lost sight of something important. Sir Richard Branson conceived of the Carbon War Room (CWR) and realized that what we actually needed was action. New technologies are important, but there are hundreds of discovered technologies that we never implemented at scale.

The Carbon War Room, for which I served as CEO from 2009 until I left in March 2012, is a Washington, DC–based nonprofit collaborative that is approaching the challenge of global carbon emissions with the platform of "climate wealth" at its center. As I mentioned in the introduction to this book, it coined the phrase "creating climate wealth."

The CWR is a global, independent nonprofit that has a mission to "harness the energy and resources of entrepreneurs to catalyze market-based approaches to climate change solutions."

Leaders of the CWR believe the data McKinsey and others have put forth, stating that "approximately 50 percent of the climate change challenge can be addressed profitably by *existing technologies*—is a business opportunity masked as a crisis." In other words, the answers already exist to meet the 2020 climate reduction goal cost effectively.

This is not a question of more innovation but rather a question of effective implementation. To deploy these proven technologies requires a systematic approach to bringing confidence to institutional capital and then engaging the right stakeholders. In the past, this was done through government expenditures and credit guarantees—something difficult to come by at $10 trillion scale today. Tracking and reporting clear measurable outcomes is also essential.

The CWR approach the challenges with climate wealth and seek to set up "markets for entrepreneurs to make money for themselves and investors…[as] the only way to achieve the response we need at sufficient speed and scale." The CWR targets the movement of institutional capital into a "working marketplace" and targets "the elimination of market inefficiencies (in the form of insufficient information and high transaction costs)." CWR recognizes that policy and technology conditions also must be addressed but feels that even in areas where they are no longer barriers, capital still is slow to flow into deployment.

So with this broad approach, CWR has adopted the "wedges" approach, which was pioneered by Princeton University's Stephen Pacala and Robert H. Socolow. Using the wedges approach requires a focus on reducing emissions by sector a gigaton at time. With each gigaton, you make steady, planned progress on the goal of saving the climate. You can prioritize gigatons based on policy, markets, capacity, social goals, or any other characteristic.

The CWR focuses on markets and cost-effectiveness. Others have also made progress, including the aforementioned McKinsey cost curve, International Energy Agency (IEA), United Nations Environment Program (UNEP), Rocky Mountain Institute (RMI), Accenture, and HSBC, to name a few.

In all of these analyses there is a similar approach, government policy needed to make it safe for institutional investors to invest with confidence. The challenge is that while investors purport to be ready, few have explained to entrepreneurs how to bridge the divide between the roadmap and the implementation.

So how did the CWR go about it? It started with creating the roadmap for success with practitioners in the sector, as mentioned above. Once we came to some consensus on the analysis, we verified their work and prioritized CWR's precious dollars on the highest impact opportunities. Finding the people within those sectors, then, who have the "scar tissue" from the difficulties of translating recommendations to results on the ground was the next big step.

Getting people who have spent the better part of their life solving one problem to be excited and engaged is not hard; not letting them down continues to be the struggle. The path becomes somewhat self-evident once the implementers are brought in, but logic is never enough. Creating momentum and buzz, usable databases with transparent information, and other tangible milestones is important.

So the first step then was to identify what the opportunity set looked like. CWR represented it with the following diagram:

With the opportunities identified, functionally the teams had to approach the challenge from three perspectives: the business opportunity, stakeholder engagement, and active operations.

1) **Business opportunity**: The Carbon War Room's research and intelligence team reviews many of the policy reports that already exist to see if it can substantiate that a gigaton-scale opportunity actually exists within current market mechanisms. Even more importantly, the team finds practitioners within the business community that might actually care about the climate change opportunity.

2) **Stakeholder engagement**: To engage all the stakeholders requires connecting them. At the CWR, network management is tasked with the essential function of engaging the key stakeholders who have the "scar tissue" and want to share their experiences productively. They have the vital role of linking "friends, founders, and funders" into an active group of engaged individuals using such offline tools as Creating Climate Wealth conferences as well as online collaborative tools CWR has created.

3) **Active operations**: This is a group who identifies and selects the sectors that best overlap with the ability to make change in the course of climate wealth creation.

Getting to $10 Trillion

When making these estimates, it is always important to remind ourselves that these are simply educated guesses. In 2012, the International Energy Agency undertook an extensive effort and concluded that an incremental $5 trillion of investment was needed and could be profitably invested versus the business-as-usual case across the world to stay on track to keeping global temperatures below two degrees. Since they only calculated the incremental investment, they defined $5 trillion of renewable electricity generation investments as part of the business-as-usual case. If we pull those investments out, we get $10 trillion of total investments.

To map the IEA estimates to the Carbon War Room categories, we made further calculated guesses, but some broad themes emerged. Given the need for a rapid ramp-up, it is clear that renewable electricity and building efficiency have to lead the way since many of the other categories simply do not have enough existing momentum. This is not because of intrinsic potential, but because moving this much capital requires trained personnel and institutional comfort. This does not mean that the investment spread has to be the same after 2020. In fact, renewable electricity and energy efficiency will probably slow in their growth, making way for the other sectors to continue to accelerate to meet the even more difficult 2030 climate change goals.

Bloomberg New Energy Finance Totals

	2010	2011	2012	2013	2014	2015	2016	2017	2018	2019	2020	Total
Bloomberg New Energy Finance Total	$ 243	$ 302	$ 269									$ 814
By Sector												
Agriculture	$ 3	$ 3	$ 3	$ 3	$ 3	$ 5	$ 7	$ 12	$ 22	$ 41	$ 51	$ 153
Energy Supply	$ 208	$ 272	$ 239	$ 274	$ 315	$ 378	$ 454	$ 545	$ 818	$ 1,226	$ 1,840	$ 6,570
Forestry	$ 1	$ 1	$ 1	$ 1	$ 1	$ 2	$ 2	$ 3	$ 5	$ 8	$ 11	$ 36
Industry	$ 3	$ 3	$ 3	$ 3	$ 5	$ 7	$ 10	$ 12	$ 17	$ 21	$ 27	$ 110
Transport and Infrastructure	$ 3	$ 3	$ 3	$ 3	$ 3	$ 5	$ 9	$ 15	$ 26	$ 47	$ 87	$ 203
Waste Management	$ 3	$ 3	$ 3	$ 3	$ 3	$ 5	$ 7	$ 10	$ 15	$ 23	$ 34	$ 109
Residential and Commerical Buildings	$ 22	$ 17	$ 18	$ 49	$ 90	$ 146	$ 221	$ 326	$ 413	$ 608	$ 910	$ 2,819
Total	$ 243	$ 302	$ 269	$ 336	$ 420	$ 546	$ 710	$ 923	$ 1,316	$ 1,974	$ 2,960	$ 10,000

Addressing climate change takes a planned, systematic approach. One important barrier to remember is "perception." Even leaders such as Germany are hard-pressed to say that such climate change solutions as solar and wind power can drive an entire economy. Without changing this perception globally, the investment above will never happen.

Creating our carbon economy was achieved piece by piece over a century. Dismantling it, while increasing our electric production, is a puzzle to solve. And, throughout time, we have always solved puzzles while creating wealth opportunities. In essence, today it is creating climate wealth.

CHAPTER SEVENTEEN:

Grid-Connected Renewable Electricity

Despite the 2008 financial downturn, the worst in the last half-century, the clean-energy sector attracted more than $1 trillion of investment from 2004 to 2011, maintaining a trajectory of a 25-percent growth rate, according to Bloomberg New Energy Finance. By 2020, clean-energy investments are expected to attract another $3 trillion.

These numbers notably demonstrate that this sector is well on track to make a difference. By 2020, 100 percent of all incremental electricity generation could come from zero-emission sources. The numbers are large enough to attract the attention of global power brokers and have been driven by commercial banks, insurance companies, and the German-owned development bank Kreditanstalt für Wiederaufbau (KFW).

The question now is, how do we make an even bigger difference by bringing in pension funds, sovereign wealth funds, and retail investors? Some thought leaders advocate for more mandates; others insist more subsidies are needed to propel this sector. But the average electricity price throughout the world ranges between ten to fifteen cents per kilo-watt-hour, and 20 percent of all electricity generated in the world is sold at prices above fifteen cents per kilowatt-hour. Offsetting this expensive electricity represents a market size of more than $3 trillion without any subsidies. With electricity rates continuing to go up because of high costs of fuel, commodities, and reliability measures, the market is only getting bigger.

Critical Vertical Market Lacks Respect

At this telling crossroads, with thousands of companies installing renewable-energy projects, deployment is taking place on a major scale, and millions of people are working in this sector. But this critical vertical market lacks respect. The global decision-makers are still not convinced that the United States, or any other nation, could be powered with solar and wind.

Why? The successful deployment of running the grid using solar, wind, and other renewable-energy sources rests upon harnessing technologies popularized since the late 1990s. For example, the Internet and mobile technologies are playing an increasing role in managing the grid. But decision-makers managing grids are still using 1960s and 1970s technology models. The obsolete "why fix something that isn't broken" mentality has thrust us into a technological quagmire. The result is that most power plants are still turned on and off with the equivalent of the landline telephone.

It's obvious that outmoded command-and-control models are no longer efficient.

Even though solar is being successfully deployed, almost all utility companies refuse to even account for their presence when managing the grid. This points to a need for respect.

It's Not about Money

Clearly, the "money talks" adage is seriously flawed. What's needed is intellectual backing. We need power brokers and top decision-makers to drive home the findings of the European Climate Foundation, US National Renewable Energy Laboratory (NREL), University of Delaware, and others that say that reaching "renewable-energy sources, accessed with commercially available technologies, could adequately supply 80% of total electricity generation in 2050, while balancing supply and demand at the hourly level" (Hand, 2012).

NREL's comprehensive findings make it abundantly clear that renewable energy has proven itself and can provide an overwhelming share of the electricity needed to power a growing, thriving economy. The study also said that this target is achievable with commercially available technology. We don't need to invent anything, but we do need fresh thinking in order to upgrade and modernize our electrical systems. That takes new business models, system planning, and recognition of new market realities. To achieve that renewable-energy target, we need to employ the same type of strategy that fueled every major strategic infrastructure upgrade in the past. The European Climate Foundation study found that the cost of reaching this decarbonized grid would be the same or less than the business-as-usual case.

That's achievable with government planning that encourages deployment at scale, not more study. Most of us saw this slow-moving train in action during the 1990s when the government was deregulating the phone system. The problem is that President Obama hasn't stood behind and advocated for NREL's findings. And neither has anyone else in power, except maybe Germany's Angela Merkel—and that support has been tepid at best. Increased support at the highest level is what it will take to achieve respect.

Make no mistake: solar, wind, and other renewables are motoring along and will attract $3 trillion in capital, but the lack of respect and planning will lead to stranded assets and higher electricity prices. All of the pieces of the infrastructure puzzle are right in front of us. But they need to be assembled.

The world wants change. What's missing is leadership.

Several banks and financial institutions would willingly invest in projects in emerging markets such as Chile, Sri Lanka, and Tanzania. These and other countries around the world are generating as much as 50 percent of their electricity with expensive diesel fuel. The economics of switching people to solar, wind, hydro, or other technologies is already profitable, but many question whether it can be made reliable.

We have the data that show these technologies are reliable across an entire system, but people need to be convinced. They want proof. They still believe that grids operate well if there is a central-station power-generating source controlled by a landline telephone. Alternative energy sources are still seen as unproven, New Age experiments. The frustrating reality is that we're way beyond the R&D testing phase. Clean technologies have proven themselves. The kinks have been ironed out, problems solved. We even have places such as Denmark, Germany, and Japan that are showing that high penetration renewables leads to far higher reliability than the multiple-day power outage experiences in Washington, DC, every year.

Germany and China have the largest number of annual solar deployments and the lowest domestic costs, according to Clean Edge, a clean-tech research and advisory firm. Those countries have created a strategy where low or falling solar-system prices fuel new deployments, which help their domestic solar industries to achieve lower costs. Germany has practically ended its subsidies by setting its solar buyback rate at a price less than the retail electricity rate. China still subsidizes deployments but views solar as a far easier way to secure the power it needs than buying more coal at more than one hundred dollars per ton from Australia.

Clean Edge's researchers said that it's difficult to identify the reasons that account for a country or company's successful deployment of solar. But they concluded that it's possible to deliver economic deployment and lower energy prices. To create that scenario, policy and leadership play an important role.

Many G20 countries (a group of 20 major economies) have piloted clean-energy programs since 1992. But it would have happened much sooner if policy-makers actually thought this future was opening up new innovation as they did with the advent of the mobile phone.

To successfully deploy clean-energy programs at scale, respect must be coupled with more government-sponsored studies and then—to reiterate— top governmental leaders must promote these solutions. The NREL study, for example, isn't enough. In the United States, people who are generally not experts in the field regulate electricity at the state level. Even young children know that renewable energy is our future, but their parents need "air cover." Leaders are conflicted about decisions they know are right in the long term, because utilities continue to tell them these changes will lead to Armageddon as local renewable energy destroys the traditional hundred-year-old monopoly utility business model. It's the change that is needed.

Consider this fact: 20 percent of electricity is sold at exorbitantly high prices. Clean-energy solutions could result in at least $3 trillion in cost-effective investment. Keep in mind that while electricity prices keep rising, renewable-energy costs keep coming down.

For solutions to scale, enthusiastic customers, especially at the government level, are needed. If the government of Kenya said that it wants to achieve a 50-percent renewable-energy goal, yet no one is instructed to sign utility-backed power purchase agreements, how would investors ever get comfortable? People have to be told to step up to the proverbial plate and make it happen.

Our electricity reliability, emission, and water problems could be solved if government just showed the way. Given the economic opportunity, there is no longer a need for subsidies, but there is a great need for respect. For example, today, many people believe that our climate change problems cannot be solved by current technology. Respect from government is needed to be able to convince investors and the general public. In reality, we could run a 100 percent renewable electricity grid.

Outrageously exorbitant energy costs are sucking the lifeblood out of the US economy. Since 1999, electricity rates for commercial customers in the United States have gone up 50 percent—that is more than $100 billion in additional payments annually by consumers and business. If that money were available in the pockets of working Americans, we would have a more robust economy.

Wouldn't that be nice?

CHAPTER EIGHTEEN:
Energy Access

Approximately 1.6 billion people, or one in every five people on earth, have no electricity.

Most of the energy-poor live in just eleven countries of the world. Ranked by the International Monetary Fund's 2011 Gross Domestic Product Per Capita report, the rankings reflect the countries with the lowest purchasing-power parity (PPP). In 2011, these non-electrified populations subsidized kerosene and diesel at the rate of $88 billion, according to the Center for Global Development. In 2012, the annual cost of global consumption of fossil-based subsidies topped $409 billion—a hefty sum, considering the number of people that have been left behind and the state of our global economy.

Cost of Energy Access

Separately, the World Bank estimates that the 1.3 billion people around the world who don't have access to energy in their homes spend $37 billion per year on subsidized energy. Amazingly, of the $88 billion governments spend on subsidies, less than 20 percent actually reaches the poor—its intended destination.

In India, when the Indian state of Bihar's chief minister, Nitish Kumar, took office in November 2005, he estimated that only 2 percent of the money allocated for programs for the poor reached their destination. Kumar was re-elected in 2010 because he was able to increase the efficacy of the program so that 40 percent of the funds allocated to the poor reached their destination.

Mobile-Phone Users Pay Usurious Prices in Off-Grid Locations

The Global System of Mobile Communications (GSM) Association reported that 543 million mobile phones are located in off-grid locations where they have no choice but to pay vendors $1.5 billion per month to charge their cell phones. At a price of twenty cents per charge, many people are paying more than five dollars per kilowatt-hour—forty-five times the average electricity price in the United States!

What's more, some 600,000 off-grid telecom towers around the world run on diesel for part of the time, with 40 percent of a telecom tower's operating expenses allocated for diesel fuel alone. The government of India, for example, spends $2.5 billion per year on diesel subsidies for the profitable telecom industry alone.

Most people using diesel are paying more than fifty cents per kilowatt-hour, four to five times the average price paid for electricity in urban areas and the rest of the developed world. In 2011, sub-Saharan Africa bought more than ten thousand megawatts of new diesel generators at a cost of some $5 billion.

This demand proves that people are willing to pay for convenient electricity, which increasingly can now come from solar, wind, biomass, hydro, or other alternative energies. Yet impact entrepreneurs face market barriers that prevent them from accomplishing their goals. A diesel engine for a telecom tower, for example, costs less than $5,000. A solar system capable of powering a telecom tower is $25,000. But the diesel engine could easily be using about three thousand gallons of diesel per year, which translates to a $12,000-annual fuel cost.

You can't argue with numbers. Over a ten-year period, solar comes in at roughly $6,000 per year with battery replacement, compared to $12,000 annually for just the subsidized diesel fuel.

If you remove the $25,000-capital expense by allowing the customer to pay for solar over time, the numbers are still undeniably appealing.

Even with 18-percent interest charges in many emerging markets, the numbers prove that it is a viable long-term solution.

The Challenge

Even though the solution seems like a no-brainer, the challenge is figuring out how to convince investors that solar—or biomass or other renewable energy solutions—makes sense. Even with all of the problems that diesel customers face—fuel theft, health issues, unpredictable maintenance costs, supply chain challenges, and other surprises—switching is not easy. Investors like diesel because, if people don't pay, they can just cut off the diesel supply. Investors are learning that you can do the same for renewable energy, but the education process is slow.

Many unsolved problems don't revolve around costs. This harkens back to an earlier chapter focusing on understanding what customers want. What they want is a twenty-four-seven solution and no angst. Yes, price matters. But the overriding issue for customers is reliability.

Energy Access, the Global Challenge

Hundreds of firms globally are focused on solving just the telecom problems, which include access, price, and electricity sources. And there are hundreds of other firms that are coping with the problem of diesel replacement for industrial facilities. Still more entrepreneurs are focused on solar lanterns and other portable power solutions for people's homes, which is also an enormous issue in the developing world. There is no shortage of companies trying to solve these problems—and they all have the same thing in common. For the most part, they have not been able to access mainstream capital. This is what is preventing the solutions from coming forth to the markets.

There are two overriding problems. One is facing these entrepreneurs who are trying to figure out how to attract mainstream capital at scale. The other is: how do we get potential customers to think beyond the moment? A service approach might work like this: "You are paying fifty cents per kilowatt-hour now. We can charge you twenty-five cents per kilowatt-hour, but you will have to sign a seven-year contract for the telecom tower."

The logic is irrefutably sound, but most entrepreneurs don't know how to attract the capital once the contract is signed—pointing to a glaring market failure in the infrastructure space. How do we ensure that contracts are standardized so they are financeable by mainstream investors?

There is no lack of money in the system. Poor people already pay $37 billion annually for energy services—the same amount of total investment to provide basic energy to the poor. This doesn't even include the government subsidies to the tune of about $88 billion, most of which is stolen or simply mismanaged by those in a position to regulate.

Here is how the numbers break down: the poor pay about $37 billion annually for inefficient energy like kerosene, charcoal, and diesel fuel. The technologies exist to replace these inefficient sources with efficient ones for less than $37 billion – a one-year payback. In addition, the poor also spend close to $1.5 billion a month just to charge their cellphones using high-cost diesel fuel. That totals $18 billion annually when existing alternate solutions could be profitably employed. An even more comprehensive solution could be deployed by creating micro-grids in surrounding the existing 600,000 diesel-fueled telecom towers. It would cost approximately $25,000 each to retrofit them, which tacks on another $15 billion in investment.

Globally, 650,000 megawatts of diesel or other oil-based products are running. To offset the 650,000 megawatts of diesel—or other oil-based burning products—would take about $1.3 trillion in investment. As of this writing, oil hovers around one hundred dollars a barrel and is expected to stay there.

Some companies have figured out how to provide energy inexpensively and profitably. One such company I have invested in is KMR Infrastructure, Inc. KMR's goal is to reduce energy costs by providing clean, high-value renewable energy on a distributed basis to developing nations employing innovative delivery models. The company is signing power-purchase agreements in Tanzania with Tanesco, the local utility company. Tanesco has about fifty megawatts of mini-grids or micro-grids fueled by diesel that service remote areas of Tanzania. Tanesco is paying more than one dollar per kilowatt-hour because the villages are so remote. KMR is writing contracts for twenty-nine cents per kilowatt-hour. The utility is saving more than 70 percent and getting reliable, renewable energy. At that price point, gasified biomass or solar can be installed and generate a fair rate of return for investors. That's a win-win for the utility and the entrepreneur, impressive proof that this kind of project can generate mainstream capital interest.

Another innovative company is Luma Light, which provides affordable, sustainable, and environmentally friendly lighting solutions for poor rural communities in West Africa's Sierra Leone.

More than 95 percent of the Sierra Leone population has no access to the electricity grid. Villagers spend almost 10 percent of their incomes on expensive and dirty solutions, mostly kerosene lamps. The destructive and potentially lethal gases emitted by these lamps contribute to the incidences of diseases that kill nearly 2 million children in developing nations each year. A room lit by kerosene can have concentrations of pollution ten times safe levels. And about 1.5 million people, mostly women, die of this pollution every year, in addition to those who die from burns in fires.

Working with entrepreneurs in rural Sierra Leone, Luma Light initially developed a test rental market of rechargeable lights for more than one hundred homes. Local entrepreneurs are given solar lights, which they rent out for a small fee to end users on a day-to-day basis. The fee is lower than an average household spends on one satchel of kerosene and enough for entrepreneurs to recoup the costs of the equipment in less than ten months. On a $1,000-investment over five years, which is the life of a lamp, an entrepreneur generates about $9,000 of revenue. That is an enormous amount of money, considering that earnings of two or three dollars a day translate to a decent income in Sierra Leone's remote rural areas.

The company's goal is to scale operations so that affordable light is available to Sierra Leone's poor. At this writing, Luma Light has reached scores of households, providing more than fifty-five hundred hours of renewable, healthful, and safe light.

These are just two examples of remarkable companies with enormous potential because the economics are fundamentally sound. Governments don't need to subsidize these solutions; they just have to convince the poor that these solutions are worth trying. By doing so, these solutions and others can be scaled to reach large populations. These technologies not only generate impressive profits, but they also can change people's lives by giving them a better standard of living.

We don't have up-to-the-minute data about how fast the solar-lamp market is growing. But by 2012, as an example, D.light, a small company with an LED solar light bulb, had served 10 million customers.

Carl Pope, environmentalist and former executive director of the Sierra Club, has said that the following ingredients are needed to light the lives of 1.2 billion people:

1. Capital to pay for solar or other renewable electrical generation for 400 million households that depend on kerosene.
2. Business models for those households to pay for the electricity they use, at the price it really costs, which is a lot less than kerosene.
3. Financing, public policy, and partnerships to create the supply chains and distribution networks capable of getting distributed electrical systems to every household that needs them (Pope, 2012).

Said Pope, "The money is on the table. It's just on the wrong plates." Here are data he presented on the "Two Flawed Ideas That Prevent Progress":

- **The Grid Fallacy**
  - We must electrify the last villages and households by building out the grid from the top down—won't work.
- **The Aid Trap**
  - Solar and other renewables are expensive, so we must "give them away" to the end users so that they can afford them.
  - Poor nations spend $80-plus billion per year subsidizing fossil fuels—more than 80 percent is "diverted" before reaching the bottom of the pyramid.

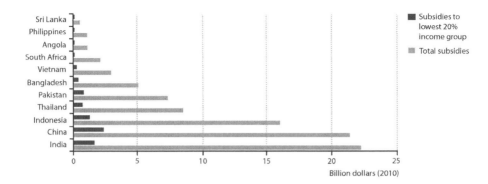

The data show how much money is currently being subsidized in poor countries where the funds do not make it to the people for the intended purpose. This information was further supported in data released by the IEA in 2011. Their report calls the grid fallacy into question, among other things. (Decentralizing the model to allow for more effective and scalable energy availability is an obvious choice.) Advocating for these solutions opens opportunities on several levels to engage millions of people with necessary services and opens huge new markets to entrepreneurs and investors globally.

CHAPTER NINETEEN:
Solutions for Achieving Building Efficiency

Since his groundbreaking 1976 essay, "Energy Strategy: The Road Not Taken?" Amory Lovins and many other energy experts have debated the best way to retrofit billions of square feet of buildings, but no one has come up with a definitive solution. It is worth working on because, aside from renewable electricity, building efficiency is the "easiest" way to take advantage of our $10-trillion investment opportunity.

We know all the components of the problem, we've identified potential solutions, and, more importantly, we know why viable solutions aren't being implemented. In short, the success of solar power and other onsite distributed generation has unlocked the key to building efficient, off-balance-sheet financing.

First, a few words on our approach to energy. Our present path is a supply-side approach (which is a hard way to deal with this issue). To meet our future energy needs, we will need to build more electricity power plants and drill more oil and gas. The supply-side approach is flawed; it's risky, vulnerable, expensive, capital-intensive, and polluting the environment.

Three decades ago, Lovins said that a long-term commitment to coal burning would cause substantial and possible irreversible changes in global climate. He had also forecast a dangerous nexus between nuclear power and nuclear weapons.

Lovins's demand-side (soft) solution, however, is gentler on the environment, society, and our pocketbooks. Rather than the hard path's (supply side) continuous increase of energy supplies, the soft path initially advocates reducing demand through energy conservation and efficiency, followed by employing distributed energy technologies such as solar, wind, and biomass to meet energy needs in renewable ways that are decentralized, diverse, and easily deployable.

Lovins's reasoning was securely grounded in the fact that half the energy produced globally is wasted. So Lovins advocated a strategy he called "least cost" by recommending meeting energy needs with "negawatts," or energy savings, because it costs significantly less to save energy than it does to make it.

Considering the global circumstances at the time, Lovins's solutions made sense. It was the mid-'70s, and we were thrust into an oil crisis when oil-producing nations imposed an embargo on the United States and its allies in response to US support for Israel during and after the Arab-Israeli War of 1973. It's hard to forget the endless gas lines that made us question our love affair with large, gas-guzzling cars.

Dan Yergin, Pulitzer Prize-winning author of *The Prize*, recently published *The Quest*, where he asserts that energy efficiency, especially the way we use energy, would be the largest resource at our disposal.

Yergin focuses on the mixture of energy resources necessary to power a growing population and economy into the future. He stresses the importance of diversifying and broadening our energy portfolio so that it supports a growing global economy. The author envisions a rebirth of renewable-energy sources and points to developments in wind technology, which have made impressive strides in recent years. Solar has incredible potential, Yergin said, but it will be achieved only when costs come down.

Yergin dubbed energy conservation the "fifth fuel." He said efficient use of energy is an important piece of the energy-security puzzle. His solution for achieving a better energy future: taking advantage of technological innovation, regulation, and cost-effective methods.

Building-Efficiency Strides

New buildings constructed over the past decade are more energy efficient than ones built in the past.

This is in part because governments have adopted and strengthened existing building codes. In the United States, this is pursued at the state level. The result is that some states have taken the issue of energy efficiency very seriously, whereas others have done little but give lip service to the efficacy of energy-saving programs.

In Oklahoma, for example, a wind turbine powers the governor's mansion. In Chicago's City Hall, workers are cooled during the summer by a sod-garden roof. And in Colorado, the state capitol in Denver is heated and lit by solar panels.

In 2008, Maryland passed the EmPOWER Energy Efficiency Act that sets targets to reduce both per capita energy consumption and per capita peak demand by 15 percent by the end of 2015 (based on a 2007 baseline). The goal of the program is to reduce the need of building unnecessary peak electricity generating plants and to extend the life of overworked substations and other expensive infrastructure. In addition to system savings, the program is anticipated to put more than $150 million back into the pockets of Maryland residents.

The Bigger Challenge: Higher Levels of Energy Efficiency

Since buildings account for about 70 percent of electricity consumption and 40 percent of greenhouse-gas emissions in the United States, energy experts strongly advocate enforcing energy codes because these codes lead to higher levels of energy efficiency. The challenge is that our old buildings are not retrofitted under these types of energy codes.

Jim Edelson, senior project manager for the New Buildings Institute, a nonprofit organization dedicated to creating model-building codes, has said that energy efficiency in buildings is the "least expensive carbon abatement."

California spearheaded a nationwide movement toward energy-smart code modification in 1978, with the adoption of Title 24—a set of high-efficiency standards and requirements for walls, roofs, windows, insulation, heating, water, lighting, and ventilating and air-conditioning systems. Coupled with mandates for energy-efficient appliances, Title 24 standards have saved Californians more than $56 billion in electrical and natural gas expenses, according to the California Energy Commission.

Although per capita electricity usage in the United States has increased by almost 50 percent since the mid-1970s, California has reportedly maintained the same per capita electricity use.

Encouraged by California's energy-conserving policies, several states have developed low-energy building codes. Even though they're a step in the right direction, they don't capture existing buildings. The result is a lot of efficient new buildings in a sea of old inefficient ones.

As a result of several states' efforts to create and enforce low-energy building codes, regulators now recognize that new buildings are on track to being more efficient, whereas existing buildings should now receive the bulk of their focus. Rather than tear down old buildings, especially the fortress-like structures built in the 1940s, it's ultimately more cost-effective to retrofit them so that they're energy efficient.

Progress Has Been Embarrassing at Best

Even though innovative energy-conserving programs get a lot of ink, energy-conservation efforts have been embarrassingly ineffective.

Utility companies have mandated rebates, and energy-efficient fluorescent bulbs have been given away as a result of subsidy programs. The EPA's Energy Star program, launched in 1992 to reduce greenhouse-gas emissions through energy efficiency, has saved about $230 billion on utility bills. But we've made little progress on building retrofits.

Fundamentally, there simply isn't enough money. Most building retrofit programs have to over subsidize efficiency because consumers simply don't make it a priority to spend money improving their homes and businesses. In short, we have not been able to attract mainstream capital in a meaningful way.

Most building owners understand the logic of spending $10,000 to realize savings of $3,333 a year. Returns in excess of 30 percent can be common for building owners considering efficiency. Even in the face of this data, many building owners simply don't think that energy efficiency matters. They ultimately refuse to prioritize and make the upfront investment when they can do other things with their money. In Washington, DC, the Sustainable Energy Utility is giving lighting systems away for free. These are systems with less than a one-year payback because they don't trust that enough consumers can be persuaded to part with even one dollar upfront.

Achievable Solutions

Solutions exist, and impressive strides are being made. New, persuasive financing approaches to energy efficiency are in the works. The Property Assessed Clean Energy (PACE) program is one such approach.

Originally created as a Special Energy Financing District or "on-tax bill solar and efficiency financing" in 2005, the program was designed to overcome the biggest barrier to solar and energy-efficiency retrofits: upfront costs. Further, both solar and energy efficiency pay dividends over at least twenty years—but financing solutions were much shorter than that. PACE enabled homeowners to "mortgage" these improvements and pay only for the benefits they derived while they owned their homes.

PACE provides upfront capital that is paid back through a special assessment on participants' property taxes. Despite the economic and environmental benefits from energy efficiency, initial costs to buy new equipment or renovate buildings have led most building owners to buy the cheapest first-cost items instead of considering life-cycle costs.

With PACE financing, property owners can take advantage of energy savings immediately while spreading the cost of improvements over several years.

Financing a PACE program is repaid through an assessment added to property taxes, as I mentioned above. But unlike charges levied by utilities, a PACE financing program is only paid for by homeowners or property owners who receive efficiency upgrades. And there is no cost to those who don't participate in the program. Another attractive feature of PACE financing is that it is tied only to the property rather than the property owner. If the property is sold, payments remain with the house, forcing the new owners who are receiving the cost-saving benefits to assume the property tax payments.

Many utilities could offer a service similar to PACE, through adjusted utility bill rates. A utility provides upfront funding, and homeowners agree to pay an extra hundred dollars a month, for example, on their electricity bills to pay them back.

Both of the programs have been well received because all parties benefit. The spillover effects are enormous because people are finally seeing that energy efficiency can be achieved cost-effectively without straining their finances.

Financing Breakthroughs

On the financing side, in the wake of many successful solar investments, customers are starting to finance large, expensive, energy-efficient air-conditioning units by negotiating third-party financing, similar to the contracts (power purchase agreements) SunEdison negotiated with customers. Instead of buying the cheapest air conditioner on the market that meets code requirements, customers can purchase more expensive energy-efficient units. Even though the unit may cost 50 percent more than cheaper units, the owner saves so much on maintenance and energy that the financed costs are almost always less expensive even after considering the higher price tag. Users not only save upfront capital, they also get quality cooling and at the same time use less electricity.

Most importantly, unlike insulation or windows, air-conditioning savings can be calculated exactly—important for potential investors. This is why investors love solar; savings are easily calculated because a meter tracks production in kilowatt-hours.

Lighting, pumps, variable speed drives, and other technology are also easily measured. In the case of lighting, energy usage can be monitored every time lights are switched on and off and also by the type of lighting source.

Building-energy systems that can be measured are more likely to be sold as a service to potential investors because there are no incalculable, unknown costs. But systems that can't be measured, such as insulation, pose problems to investors because energy savings can't be accurately assessed. The best we can do is to make educated guesses. It's not that the engineering is complicated; it's because there is no way to know whether enough insulation was blown into a commercial or residential building.

Another unknown is the effect the number of people living in a building will have on energy consumption. Two people living in a house, for example, will use far less energy than eight people.

On the financing side, however, complications arise in meeting the rigid requirements of the Financial Accounting Standards Board (FASB). The FASB has established guidelines addressing which technologies can be included as off-balance-sheet services and which ones cannot. The result is that we're significantly restricted as to which ones qualify and which don't. This is an important issue that has to be addressed because CFOs want these types of contracts to show up on the income statement as "energy services," not on the balance sheet as a "loan." Both CEOs and CFOs find energy efficiency rarely to be a core competency worthy of their precious internal capital investments—even if energy-saving technologies significantly reduce costs.

Good Ideas Are Not Enough

At this critical juncture, we must acknowledge that the power of a good idea, whether it's building energy efficiency or renewable energy, is not enough. Blogger, entrepreneur, and programmer Derek Sivers has said: "Ideas are just a multiplier of execution. Execution is worth millions."

Sivers was low-balling execution's importance. From my perspective, it could be worth trillions.

The power of a brilliant idea only comes when you can prove beyond any doubt that it works. In building efficiency, this has been the Achilles' heel over and over. The technology works, but the sales and marketing model continues to fail. This is why it's so important to make sure that these off-balance-sheet, energy-efficient technologies have measurement-verification systems built into them. With that enhancement, energy efficiency can be measured like solar was to the multibillion-dollar solar finance industry.

The disturbing conclusion is that energy efficiency is not one technology. It's a series of technologies with different characteristics—lighting, air conditioning, control systems, insulation, and many others. They are all important in new building construction, but for building retrofits you really have to narrow the field to those that can be financed by mainstream solar investors.

New Advances in Building-Management Systems

Building-management system (BMS) technologies are not new. What is new and exciting is that they have improved notably during the past decade. That's important, considering that as soon as a building is constructed, it goes off spec, meaning it no longer meets specifications and requirements or is partially obsolete. Even though state-of-the-art heating and air-conditioning systems are installed, it's only a matter of time before systems start to fail. For any number of reasons, building systems stop performing optimally.

With advances in the Web and mobile phone technologies combined with more sophisticated BMSes, buildings can be monitored around the clock so that they run according to specifications. Companies such as BuildingIQ and others have created technologies that not only monitor buildings' energy systems but also can troubleshoot potential problems. They can find trouble spots and glitches affecting performance and fix them before they escalate into crippling problems. Imagine the impact of a power outage in a building that houses thousands of people. By taking all energy precautions, companies can take advantage of savings of 7 to 10 percent just by making sure its buildings function according to specifications.

The impetus for improved BMS technologies is the increased complexity of new buildings, according to Greenbiz.com. Buildings now have energy and sustainability systems, such as rainwater harvesting, exterior shading, water reclamation, and sun-tracking systems, to name a few. The challenge is making sure these sophisticated systems function at peak efficiency.

In an article in architectmagazines.com, Michael Tatoyan, a senior mechanical engineer at engineering design firm Stantec, Inc., stressed the management aspect in BMS. Tatoyan said BMSes have capability. "You can tell them how to behave and decide things based on conditions," he said.

Tatoyan also said that thinking systems are becoming the norm on high-performance systems. Owners can "control a building to its actual needs and will give designers data for what works and what doesn't."

Tatoyan added, "Though automation systems exist primarily on larger commercial and institutional projects today, in the not-too-distant future, these are going to be code-minimum buildings."

Government Green-Lights Funds for Upgrading Building Efficiency

The General Services Administration awarded IBM a contract to install low-cost, high-value networked technologies in fifty of the federal government's most energy-intensive buildings. Building-management systems will be connected to a central, Cloud-based platform, which will significantly improve energy efficiency and save approximately $15 million in taxes annually. When the system is completed, the buildings' tenants will be able to view the performance of their buildings on public dashboards and see an analysis of energy savings, along with recommendations for increasing efficiencies.

The last critical component essential to achieving building efficiency—making the $10-trillion opportunity achievable—is to change the way utilities think about energy savings in homes so they meet the reliability needs of the grid. Instead of creating more capacity by upgrading transmission lines and substations, the utilities need to find ways to help customers use significantly less energy.

We have the technologies and the expertise necessary to achieve energy efficiency. The missing component is a strategic plan that evaluates and prioritizes the technologies for reaching our goals at scale.

CHAPTER TWENTY:
Why Is Industrial Efficiency So Hard?

In 1998, I worked as a contractor to the Department of Energy, working mainly on alternative transportation fuels. My colleague worked on industrial efficiency, producing roadmaps for industry sectors such as steel, aluminum, cement, fertilizer, refineries, manufacturing, and the list goes on. In 1998, we had very low cost energy by historical standards. Since that time, oil prices have increased by five times and electricity by at least 1.7 times. I always thought industrial efficiency would be easy. I was wrong.

You would think that industrial customers care about energy use since it is so much a part of the production paradigm. And in fact they do. As opposed to commercial buildings, industrial facilities use much more energy, and senior management takes energy costs very seriously. So if we have roadmaps to success and serious senior management, what's the issue?

As usual, it's never one thing. The first issue is the age-old "precious capital" argument. Every year there is a fight for capital, and almost every time these projects are prioritized based on "core competencies" of the firm. For industrial firms, energy should be higher on this list—but it rarely is. So, again, many combined heat and power projects and other upgrades have to wait until a year when the firm is flush with cash and lacking in projects to take up. They just don't make it to the top of the list as much as they should.

You might ask, why can't you use the third-party ownership model? Good question. You can, but there is a wrinkle with industrial facilities.

Every industrial customer I have ever talked to has a fervent belief that their factory is just full of "proprietary processes" and that if I owned something that resided inside the same facility, I might steal valuable insights I could sell elsewhere. They were fine with solar panels and wind farms, but industrial efficiency is more problematic because of this concern.

Then you have the "not invented here" syndrome; unfortunately, many industrial companies are very conservative and traditional, and change does not come easy to them. As opposed to commercial buildings, industrial companies are proud of their energy history. Industrial companies know that energy matters, and the engineers that work there have usually been instrumental at driving change in energy consumption. The companies have often moved from coal to fuel oil and from fuel oil to natural gas. The engineers themselves introduced electronic controls and variable speed drives. They personally attend the conferences and have chaired the working group for ASHRAE, ASME, IEEE, or whatever other alphabet soup comes their way.

The last thing they welcome is some outsider telling them how to use energy when they "invented" how to use energy. Industrial companies also have a habit of choosing CEOs who have been with the company for more than thirty years, so they are all singing from the same age-old songbook as the energy engineers because they came up the ranks with them. The interesting thing is that they always want to meet with you—just in case you come bearing gifts of information so diabolical and radical that they haven't heard it before. But that rarely happens. As it turns out, industrial customers are no different from anyone else—they have a deployment problem.

However, there are some interesting and noteworthy cases in the industrial efficiency industry that are demonstrating to others, including me, a renewed interest in the challenges to overcome, and solutions to offset waste and overconsumption.

One massive example is the Mexican company, CEMEX (www.cemex. com). CEMEX was incorporated in 1906 and is one of the largest building material suppliers in the world. It produces, distributes, and markets cement, ready-mix concrete, aggregates, and other materials to customers in more than fifty countries.

CEMEX's cement factory remains as much as 20 percent less efficient than the worst in China, and yet, rather than deploy a solution for that critical issue, they built a wind turbine in California to offset some of their consumption. Why? Because it is off-balance-sheet, and it is easier to build a wind project than to deal with the efficiency issues. I am not trying to sound cynical; it is the truth. Dealing with a project that involved thirty-five temporary jobs and installing the wind turbine is much easier for them to implement than process assessment and improvement in a company of their size.

On a positive note, however, the turbine is a 1 MW turbine with better-than-average production due to a superior power curve. Its production (1,808,000 kilowatts per hour) is the equivalent to what would be required to power more than 203 average American households and will eliminate approximately fifteen hundred tons of carbon emissions. So that is good, but isn't it kind of a Band-Aid solution?

CEMEX set a goal to reduce carbon emissions by 25 percent per ton of cement by 2015 (from a 1990 baseline) and reducing NOx emissions by 2015 from 2005 levels. They have already made significant progress reducing carbon emissions by 20.5 percent. They have plans to add four additional turbines as part of two different projects in Victorville, California, which will bring the company's total distributed wind-generating capacity in the state to more than 7 MW. It is real progress and represents real opportunity, but it still pales in comparison to the efficiency opportunities they could be addressing for even greater impact.

Another interesting example is a company called Empower Energies (www.empowerenergies.com). I am intimately familiar with this company as I am an investor and board member. Empower Energies originates, develops, designs, builds, and finances solar projects for commercial/industrial clients, institutions, and governmental entities. They target projects in the 500 kW –10 MW range. What is so interesting about them? They are sponsored by, none other than, General Motors.

Empower Energies has designed and developed solar electric vehicle charging stations for General Motors's facilities and dealerships, which they have trademarked "Green Zone®." They continue a marketing initiative that has now targeted the three thousand Chevrolet dealerships in the United States. They are also working on clean transport-focused clients, such as Toyota, which has a program they are deploying to their nationwide dealerships.

Milestones for the young company have been significant as they are becoming a leading renewable energy services platform that is designed to leverage synergies and complementarities between the commercial-scale photovoltaics (PV) and clean infrastructure markets. Their strategic partnership with GM, under which they provide the roof and ground mount solar PV projects for its global facilities and clean transportation infrastructure for Chevrolet dealers, gives them huge reach to approximately 150 facilities globally, including eighty in the United States, with pipeline potential of more than 500 MW.

Finally, we see success with the company MPC Energy (www.mpcener-gyllc.com). Based near Saint Louis, MPC Energy may be the standard-bearer in energy management systems. With more than thirty years' experience and more than three hundred customers, MPC has solidified a means by which customers reduce their energy cost by reducing the amount of energy required per unit item produced. Offering permanent enterprise energy management, their model is accurate to within 1 percent per year. It is the foremost company that has developed energy management in the industrial sector, and it had the foresight to look at decreasing energy consumption (costs) before those costs were volatile or even considered a cost variable that could be decreased.

Whereas some people accept energy management to be a supply-side question (trying to minimize purchasing), and others think of energy management as implementing several capital-based engineering projects in the hope that there will be a return on investment on the back-side. MPC has a different approach altogether. MPC believes that managing the systems and controlling how and why energy is used is the key. By working closely with clients as a third party, they can benchmark a company's energy efficiency against competitors, essentially using their bravado against them or at least as a motivator.

Rather than offering a snapshot through a one-time energy audit, MPC's continuous commissioning process allows companies to see an ongoing picture offering multiple opportunities to address consumption and wastage issues. It is a more robust approach and one that its clients are overwhelmingly satisfied with based on customer feedback.

For my part, what I see through all of these examples from CEMEX to Empower Energies to MPC is that the solutions are there, and the opportunity is significant in the industrial efficiency sector. These are not far-flung challenges that we cannot meet, but rather they are real opportunities to improve industrial efficiency by both implementing new ideas with existing technologies—such as the wind turbine for CEMEX—and finding new ways to build partnerships, such as what we see with Empower Energies and GM, to allow traditional manufacturing a way to improve their efficiency by creating new business models. And finally, through MPC, we see a better way to assess, use, and minimize waste so that efficiency is improved throughout multiple processes.

These opportunities merely scratch the surface of what is possible right now. The potential is staggering. Motivated entrepreneurs and investors can find opportunity now with some research and begin to capitalize on them right away if they so choose. It's time.

CHAPTER TWENTY-ONE:

Shipping Puts the -ization in Globalization

Ships carry more than 85 percent of the world's cargo. Mention a product—from bicycles, computers, tanks, jet fighters, and farm machinery to cellphones and automobiles—and it's probably transported around the globe by sea.

With more than ninety thousand ships traveling the seas each year, shipping is one of the most efficient ways of transporting cargo. Yet it is also one of the dirtiest industries on the globe, accounting for about 3.3 percent of the world's carbon dioxide output, according to the International Maritime Organization (IMO), and a larger amount of the soot that caused cancer in people and accelerated melting of the Arctic caps.

"If shipping were a nation, it would be the sixth-largest emitter, sandwiched between Japan and Germany," wrote Michael Kanellos on Ecomagination.com. "But don't blame the captain," he added. "Transporting goods is a natural consequence of modern life."

The industry's challenge is reducing fuel consumption and greenhouse gases without affecting world trade. We have the technology that can accomplish that goal and pay back more than $200 billion in ship upgrades in less than three years from fuel savings alone. Even the conservative IMO estimates that by 2050, ships could be at least twice as efficient as they are today and emit 35 percent to 70 percent fewer greenhouse gases because of stronger regulations. Just a 30-percent efficiency boost could save at least $70 billion a year in fuel costs. Achieving 70-percent fuel savings would take more technology, and a three-year payback isn't possible. But 30-percent savings is possible with a three-year payback.

Why the Shipping Industry Hasn't Made Fuel Efficiency a Priority

The industry has the economic resources to make fuel efficiency a priority but has done little to achieve fuel-efficiency goals because ship owners don't pay for fuel. Fuel is a pass-through to cargo owners, and they have no way to distinguish fuel-efficient from non-fuel-efficient ships. If they did, they'd certainly choose the most fuel-efficient vessels.

The result is ships are not rented based upon their fuel efficiencies, and there is no incentive for ship owners to spend millions of dollars to upgrade their ships.

The solution is to create a rating system similar to the ENERGY STAR program developed by the US Environmental Protection Agency and the US Department of Energy in 1975 to save consumers and businesses money by buying energy-efficient products and encouraging energy-saving practices.

Such a system could rate ships based upon their fuel efficiency so cargo owners would choose the most fuel-efficient ships. In 2011, the Carbon War Room (CWR) created a website, http://shippingefficiency. org, that provides efficiency ratings for more than sixty thousand of the world's container ships, tankers, bulk carriers, cargo ships, cruise ships, and ferries. Retailers, insurers, and others can select shippers committed to improving their sustainability. As of the publishing of this book, the Carbon War Room estimates that its work has fundamentally changed the profitability of inefficient "G" grade ships by shifting a full 2 percent of the volume they used to receive to more efficient ships.

The CWR also provided other fuel-saving recommendations, such as slow steaming or going more slowly, that can significantly cut fuel usage. Danish shipping giant Maersk, for example, recently reportedly annual savings of approximately $300 million on diesel fuel by slow steaming.

CWR researchers also published data advising ship owners to try to fully rent their ships because earnings were significantly higher for ships that travel full as opposed to those traveling at 70-percent capacity. This information helped shippers choose ships that were better utilized over ships that were underutilized. The more efficient ships are significantly more profitable than ships that were traveling at less than full capacity.

As a result of the CWR'S energy-saving efforts, the International Maritime Organization (IMO) created a mandatory Energy Efficiency Design Index (EEDI) for the manufacture of new ships. The EEDI led to a standard that requires a minimum level of energy efficiency in ship design, starting with 10-percent improvement for ships built between 2015 and 2019, 20 percent between 2020 and 2024, and 30 percent for new ships delivered after 2024. The regulation went into effect January 1, 2013.

The IMO also announced a program that helps owners improve efficiency and reduce fuel consumption of existing ships. The combined mandatory and voluntary standards could reduce industry CO_2 emissions by 23 percent by 2030.

Reducing Consumption of Bunker Oil

The changes spurred by the CWR and the IMO are expected to save almost $70 billion a year by 2020, which means ships will use less bunker oil, the dirtiest and most polluting fuel available. In contrast with quality marine diesel fuel, bunker oil is the cheapest fuel on the planet, costing pennies per gallon. The tar-like bunker fuel is so heavy that ships' pipes must be heated so that the fuel flows and doesn't get stuck or caught in the pipes.

The world's ninety thousand ships consume a mind-boggling 7.29 million barrels of bunker oil each day, or more than 84 percent of all exported oil production from Saudi Arabia, the world's largest oil exporter.

Because bunker oil is so dirty, most ships vent or exhaust it under the ship so the dangerous pollutants are not seen.

The popular phrase "out of sight, out of mind" couldn't be more appropriate. But the notion that something is quickly forgotten or dismissed as unimportant or irrelevant because we don't see it doesn't hold much credence to environmentalists and ecologists who have been monitoring the effects of bunker oil and similar pollutants for decades.

Several years ago, the British newspaper *The Guardian* reported research findings that one large container ship emits cancer- and asthma-causing pollutants equivalent to 50 million cars. That means that just twenty of these ships produce as much negative health effects as the world's one billion cars. Other noteworthy findings included the fact that the cheap bunker fuel used by the world's ninety thousand cargo ships contains close to two thousand times the amount of sulfur compared to diesel fuel used in automobiles.

The marked increase in global trading of manufactured goods has spurred development of a new breed of outsized container ships, which consume fuel not by gallons, but by tons per hour. Today, shipping accounts for more than 90 percent of global trade by volume.

By way of example, Maersk owns eight identical super-size cargo ships, which are thirteen hundred feet (397.7 meters) long and can carry 15,200 shipping containers around the globe at a steady 25.5 knots (47.2 kilometers per hour, 29.3 miles per hour). To achieve that speed, Maersk designed special extra-powerful diesel engines. One of the eight ships, the *Emma Maersk*, boasts the world's largest reciprocating engine. Five stories tall and weighing twenty-three hundred tons, the fourteen-cylinder turbocharged two-stroke behemoth puts out 84.4 MW (114,800 hp) or close to 90 MW when the motor's waste-heat recovery is factored in. These enormous engines consume about sixteen tons of fuel per hour, or more than 380 tons per day, while at sea—a massive rate of consumption.

The Real Work Is Ahead

As the CWR and IMO are making significant progress, we see a goal in sight. Improving fuel efficiency across the global fleet could save the industry up to seventy billion dollars a year in fuel costs. And measuring fuel efficiency of vessels would incentivize retrofitting of efficiency technologies to ships. It would also significantly increase investment and job growth and at the same time reduce marine greenhouse-gas emissions by up to two hundred and twenty million tons annually.

But there is much to be done before these toxic-emission goals are reached. Because only a handful of ship builders are investing in pollution-curbing technology, ship emissions, especially in international waters, is one of the least-regulated parts of our global transportation system. Shipping remains the world's biggest transport polluter.

What's Next?

In October 2012, Cargill, Huntsman Corporation, and UNIPEC UK pledged to not use any ships in the bottom third of the efficiency rating system. That means that these ships receive less business and efficient ships receive more business.

We have the data, the technology, the investment incentive, and the human resources to improve energy efficiency and significantly reduce toxic emissions. All that's needed is entrepreneurial muscle, spurred by government support, to overcome the inertia in the industry to make it part of the trillion-dollar opportunity.

CHAPTER TWENTY-TWO:
Personal Cars

It was President George W. Bush who said that the United States "is addicted to oil," but when we get down to the facts, the reality is that we are addicted to our cars. Americans love their vehicles. We love the status associated with them. We love the freedom they provide. Our cars have always had their own personas. There was a time when people identified themselves by the brand. Are you a Ford guy or a Chevy girl?

Some of that is changing. The youngest generations now leaving college and entering the workforce seem to be deferring automobile purchases. It is not clear if that is because they are too strapped with college debt to take on more, or if there is an environmental impetus, but in that demographic purchase rates are declining. For the rest of us, however, cars remain essential, it seems.

And since the 1970s, when we had the oil crisis and the gasoline shortages, we have focused on vehicle efficiency as the main indicator of success in improving our situation. This is like making a coal plant more efficient. It might make us feel better, but it is not necessarily having a substantial impact on climate emissions.

It is a simple economics issue that must be resolved. Cars are inherently a bad investment. Everyone knows that they depreciate the moment they are driven off of the lot. Cars are expensive to buy and to operate. But if you ask the average American how much they spend per day on their car, few will know. Because few will know what the hard cost is (fuel, maintenance, insurance, parking, and so on), it is hard to make an argument in favor of another option.

Let's break it down a bit. Assume a commute of one hour per day. If the average commuter does that roughly three hundred days a year, that breaks down to 3.4 percent of the year behind the wheel of a car. Most of the rest of the time, the car sits and idly collects dust. This is the worst use of an asset in the history of time! If we assume that there are 10 million new cars sold in the country annually at the (low) average cost of $20,000 each, this amounts to $200 billion in new assets just sitting. People want to save money, and most know that cars are a big savings area, but we have to change the way people evaluate and buy "mobility services" if we are to improve in this sector.

One key point that is important to make is that for all of the innovation being done for alternative engine solutions, there is a ridiculously high barrier to entry in the automotive industry. Unless one of the major car companies buys into the idea, there is little chance to get these types of innovations to market. An individual has very little chance of manufacturing anything that would actually compete with the major automotive companies unless he or she created a large fortune at PayPal first.

Existing car companies believe that they have cutting-edge innovation on engine technology already, but it takes real money to bring these solutions to market – money they don't have to spend if consumers are satisfied with the current engines already in production. Why cannibalize their own sales if there isn't a competitor breathing down their neck threating their core business. Keep in mind, by the way, that most auto companies do not consider themselves car companies as much as they do engine companies. There is a big distinction in that the engine is central to what differentiates the vehicle. It is their production pride and joy.

This is another area where government actually could step in and make a difference. In the United States right now, we just do not have an infrastructure in place that allows transportation innovators to test their ideas if the big automotive companies don't buy in.

You can circumvent many regulatory (though not safety) standards if you build *only* your own car. So, let's say you have an engine innovation or some other significant vehicle improvement. You can build that car and use it. But no matter how many people think it is great or how many say they want one, you cannot build a second car for someone else's use. Maybe you could sneak a couple out, but eventually Uncle Sam would figure it out. What if government changed the regulations and allowed you to make and sell up to two thousand of your vehicles? This two-thousand-vehicle exemption would allow you to prove your concept and attract financing. Radical idea, perhaps, but this is exactly what is possible in the electricity industry; why not the auto industry?

What about the self-propelled vehicles Google is working to develop? Crazy stuff from science fiction? No, not at all. As of fall 2012, these vehicles had logged more than 300,000 miles without a single accident. Here is what Google had to say in a press release last year: "Our vehicles, of which about a dozen are on the road at any given time, have now completed more than 300,000 miles of testing. They've covered a wide range of traffic conditions, and there hasn't been a single accident under computer control."

The company elaborates further by saying, "We're encouraged by this progress, but there's still a long road ahead. To provide the best experience we can, we'll need to master snow-covered roadways, interpret temporary construction signals and handle other tricky situations that many drivers encounter. As a next step, members of the self-driving car team will soon start using the cars solo—rather than in pairs—for things like commuting to work. This is an important milestone, as it brings this technology one step closer to every commuter. One day we hope this capability will enable people to be more productive in their cars. For now, our team members will remain in the drivers' seats and will take back control if needed."

Larry Burns, former corporate vice president of research and development for General Motors, has said that distracted drivers exist because most people believe that talking on their cellphones, texting, shaving, eating, or engaging in other tasks are more important than keeping their eyes on the road. How many people would pay to get that time back through a self-propelled vehicle? Further, Burns surmises that the cost of operating a vehicle is close to fifty dollars per hour when you include the value of the driver's time. Through self-propelled vehicles, appropriately sized vehicles and less overall vehicles, his estimate is that people could go from fifty dollars per hour to less than five dollars. A 90-percent reduction in mobility costs is a really big deal—not to mention all the savings on road construction that could be recognized if these mobility efficiencies translated to having fewer cars on the road.

What is at the heart of this particular issue is the disconnect among ideas, commercialization, and deployment. Changes to the "menu" of options are needed, regulatory intervention is needed, and different models of consumption are also needed if we are to streamline this wildly inefficient sector. Because transportation is such a big investment for government and individuals, it is worth careful consideration.

We see increasing success with companies such as Zipcar and SideCar. Both have addressed a significant gap in urban vehicle ownership. In the Zipcar model, users join a club and pay a flat rate for membership that allows them access to a vehicle when needed. This alleviates the burden of individual ownership, solves the need for personal transportation, and reduces the number of vehicles in highly congested cities and urban areas. Zipcar has operations now in fifty-plus cities (and universities) in North America and the United Kingdom. Zipcar was just acquired by Avis; let's hope Avis integrates into Zipcar instead of the other way around.

SideCar, a relatively new company, elevates the taxicab experience by allowing users to request a vehicle using an app on their smartphone. After establishing an account, they can use the app to request a vehicle; they get picked up by a driver looking for a second income and are taken wherever they need to go. Users rate drivers; drivers rate users. It is easy and efficient. It is a glorified version of car sharing and, again, solves that need for personal transportation service on demand. The company is having success quickly and is spreading.

There are some regulatory issues faced in some markets by others trying to enter this transportation space. Resistance from the existing taxi and limousine industry has been significant. Once resolved, however, this could be a promising new model for on-demand transportation.

Similar models could be used for on-demand public transportation with fuel-efficient or clean technology-powered vans or small buses to get more people going in the same general direction to share one vehicle. This is a concept known as "slugging." A smartphone app could tell you when a vehicle will be in your vicinity, and you could walk to meet it.

The bottom line is that the innovation level in the transportation sector is far behind the electricity sector. It is too bad that when we think about true automobile entrepreneurs, the last real game-changer was Henry Ford in 1903!

There is even a convergence between transportation and electricity today. Whereas most people are obsessed with electric cars, I am more curious about how valuable electric vehicle batteries are to the electric grid. Because we have agreed that cars remain parked nearly 95 percent of the time, what could we do with that power? When I look at business model innovation for this segment of the market, I can count at least seventeen revenue streams for which you could be paid significant revenues with an electric battery on top of the expected car payment.

Let's look at California as an example because it seems to be leading on renewable electricity and electric cars. In California, peak demand for electricity is approximately sixty thousand megawatts, and the grid must stay at sixty hertz to keep things running smoothly. If there were 250,000 electric cars (out of the total of 30 million registered vehicles) at twenty kilowatts apiece, these electric cars can provide about 5,000 MW of immediate power or one-twelfth of the entire grid of storage. Using 10 percent of all cars, you could back up the entire grid for a short period of time and support 100-percent renewable energy penetration.

We need to change the way we view the electric batteries in cars for what they really are—distributed sources of energy storage for the grid that just happen to be on four wheels. We need to think of mobility service contracts and not just vehicle purchases; the automobile industry could become part of the solution for the energy industry.

As is the case in other areas we have already discussed, more technology is not the answer for transportation. The deployment of existing technologies in the personal transportation sector does not currently demand more technology or more innovation on the product side. What we need to do is balance the role of government and regulation to get some latitude for scalable deployment and good manageable goals. Once we set the ground rules, the government can get out of the way and let entrepreneurs create new business models to deploy profitable products.

The answers really are right in front of us, and there are no significant missing pieces. We just need to get the right mix of government inspiration to drive the engine of capitalism down the path of creative problem-solving to identify exciting, lucrative impact opportunities for motivated entrepreneurs and business leaders to execute.

CHAPTER TWENTY-THREE:

Will Heavy Trucking Ever Care about Fuel Costs?

T. Boone Pickens Jr. launched the *Pickens Plan* during the presidential election of 2008. Both Republicans and Democrats immediately embraced it as a fantastic way to free the country from foreign oil and invest in domestic natural gas. In the years since that plan was presented, natural gas prices have plummeted, and diesel prices have returned back to roughly four dollars per gallon. There are some bright spots with Navistar, Peterbilt, Caterpillar, and Freightliner producing natural gas–powered trucks for their new truck buyer customers. Shell and Chesapeake Energy are building out natural gas refueling stations as well. But what will it take to capitalize fully on this opportunity?

We have 8.5 million heavy trucks on the road today, and the US trucking industry was expected to spend in excess of $155 billion on fuel in 2012 (Trimble 2012). Today, natural gas costs the equivalent of two dollars per gallon—about 50 percent less than diesel fuel. This spread provides less than a two-year payback on investment for most truckers.

But as we have discussed throughout this book, that is 1.8 years too long for many truck owners. For one thing, if you are an individual buyer of a brand-new truck who might have to sell it before the end of its life, you will get a whole lot of grief from your leasing company. They don't know what the trucks will be worth used, and they don't want to take the risk. Another problem is maintenance. If your truck breaks down in the middle of nowhere, will the local mechanic have the knowledge to rebuild the engine or have the spare parts on hand?

On the efficiency side, the Carbon War Room issued a report that looked at a subset of proven technologies—five physical technologies and two information and communications technologies (ICT). These technologies would cost about $30,000 per Class-8 truck, reduce fuel consumption by about 30 percent, and save about $26,400 per year. The math adds up to about an eighteen-month payback including a high interest rate. The physical technologies include aerodynamic improvements, anti-idling devices, traction and rolling resistance upgrades, transmission alternations, and automatic cruise control devices. ICT technologies use "big data" being gathered in cutting-edge ways and include such things as making sure drivers are driving safely, dynamically checking to see that the truck is maintained correctly, checking to see if anyone is stealing fuel while the driver is sleeping, calculating in real time the results of fuel savings measures so they can be customized for their fleet, and sending accurate data to investors to enable performance-based financing.

Because fuel is one of the largest expenses for both trucks owners and cargo owners (people who rent trucks), you would think that someone would care about accelerating these solutions. The US Department of Energy has been studying these opportunities since the 1970s and has the detailed reports to prove it, and the Clean Cities program has been educating fleet owners like municipalities and retailers. What gives?

For municipalities, it all comes down to money. They budget every year, and technologies that don't have a quick payback can't be put into the operating budget. The capital budget comes from bond offerings, and that money is needed for new buildings and essential repairs. For the independent truckers, many of them pass the fuel costs to the cargo owner, so they don't really care. If they spend $30,000 to upgrade their truck, the cargo owners would keep the $26,400 in fuel savings, so they need a new contract that lets them keep the savings. For the cargo owners, they should just pick trucks that are more fuel efficient, but if they don't ship enough to own a dedicated truck then there is no transparent information included in the rental platform that lets them choose a truck by efficiency and fuel type (i.e., natural gas).

So let's go through and figure out the prize for caring about this sector. Assuming that about $155 billion in fuel was used in 2012 in the United States alone, and 30 percent could be saved through efficiency, the prize is about $50 billion in investment. On the natural gas side, you get roughly the same economics, $30,000 more in investment and roughly the same amount of savings per year. So there is another $50 billion of investment, probably more, once you include the refueling stations and natural gas infrastructure upgrades. So the US market alone could deploy $100–$150 billion at an interest rate of 18 percent over a three- to five-year financing period. The truckers and cargo owners save money from day one, and consumers are protected from future price spikes from diesel fuel by diversifying the fuel mix.

There are certainly some solutions out there. With the advent of big data, we have the ability to mandate that the truckers simply report their average fuel economy results from the past six months to potential customers. Fuel-efficient trucks get rented more often and therefore are more profitable. Not easy to mandate, but the technology exists and can be deployed very quickly.

For folks buying a new truck, you can set standards so that people are forced to buy efficient trucks. Or you could work with the leasing companies to figure out their hang-up on providing competitive financing solutions for natural gas vehicles. The data exist but are buried in someone's computer. Fleet owners can work together to share the data with leasing companies to get them comfortable with fuel savings predictions and therefore used truck values. A lot of this stuff comes down to trust. This is where the government can play a key role without spending a lot of money. People would trust government data if they were engaged in the process ensuring that the government is collecting the right data.

This is also a place where third-party models could work. You could imagine that a city could convert all of its vehicles with commonsense efficiency and alternative fuel conversions cost effectively. The city could sign a ten-year diesel procurement contract with a third party for a price consistent with the market and volumes from the previous year. The third party would pay for all of the upgrades that made financial sense and calculate the amount of money it saved the city each year. Those savings would be shared with the city the following year based on transparent calculations to give the third party a 12-percent rate of return—high enough for it to take the risk with a high-credit customer such a city (consider the fact that cities have been going bankrupt in recent years). Over time, the city would save money, lower harmful emissions, reduce costly accidents, and inspire other fleets to convert with the third party, creating local economic development. While the savings are important, other factors are probably even more important to mayors. Further, the third party could be the local gas utility. They already own the local gas infrastructure and have the lobbyists to get the deal signed. These companies are generally sleepy, 2-percent growth companies. This is a way for them to double that growth rate while helping the city they care about.

Good ideas matter, but action matters more. The reason the *Pickens Plan* didn't get implemented at speed and scale is that we need an army of entrepreneurs that does the selling work locally. This is where the solar industry has really done a much better job than other sectors. Everyone is always waiting for the Fortune 500 Company to lead the charge, but they just don't make the investment necessary. And most Fortune 500 companies do not lead the way on innovation. Local entrepreneurs with a profit motive are needed to browbeat local city officials and truck owners, one at a time.

These opportunities are huge economic development opportunities. The Carbon War Room also estimates that in the United States alone, the carbon savings by 2020 could be more than 400 million tons of CO_2— not too shabby. Countries around the world are literally spending all of their hard currency importing expensive diesel fuel. Instead they could be using these efficiency and alternative fuel solutions to leverage local skills to put people back to work.

Gigaton scale often seems daunting, but when a billionaire such as Pickens is pushing on the messaging side, governments are pulling on the moral side, business is pulling on the customer side, and entrepreneurs are pushing on the solutions side, it is possible in a very short period of time. Mix in green banks, high oil prices, and civil unrest seen every day from frustrated truck drivers, and you have yourself momentum.

CHAPTER TWENTY-FOUR:
Agriculture

Few people think about what a massive industry farming is and how it can be improved. In the United States, the energy used in moving water is substantial. We use fertilizers that come from other countries; more than 54 percent of nitrogen and 85 percent of potash supply in the United States were imported in 2011. We have huge industrial farms that rely on all kinds of heavy equipment, most running on expensive diesel fuel. Equipment that processes the food uses tremendous amounts of energy. And then the food is transported by land across the country. In some inner cities, however, fresh produce is virtually impossible to find.

Joel Salatin published a new book in fall 2012 called *Folks, This Ain't Normal*, where he examines how we regard food and comments on how disconnected we have become from our food. It is a far cry from how most of the rest of the world eats, shops, and thinks about the food they consume. Most Americans are accustomed to going into giant sterile stores and buying food that has been processed, washed, sorted, and wrapped in plastic. We do not realize how different that food looks and tastes from the natural products that came out of the ground or came from the natural component ingredients.

Produce is especially troublesome. For most of us, the fruit and vegetables we consume were harvested several days earlier and processed and then transported from the farm to the grocery warehouse to the store. Few people realize that 70 percent of the cost of the produce they buy is from transportation costs—that's nearly three-quarters. The more water-heavy the produce, such as lettuce and tomatoes, the greater the transportation costs. We don't really think about this because this is the only model most urban and suburban people know. What if there were better or different ways?

What we try to do throughout this book is show, where possible, how innovation and creativity, applied correctly and with tenacity, can address problems and challenges and alleviate them while creating new opportunities and improving the issue at hand. Such is the case here in the agriculture sector with a new company called BrightFarms, a company in which I have personally invested.

New York-based BrightFarms took a model that has been around for more than twenty-five years and reapplied it to this issue. The model of hydroponic greenhouses has been used widely but never as BrightFarms is doing it. BrightFarms is partnering with cities that are looking at urban redevelopment project areas and putting these hydroponic greenhouses close to grocery stores, sometimes directly on the rooftops.

Think about it. Instead of paying to have vegetables trucked in from a huge industrial farm, this helps address our growing interest in and demand for local, sustainable food. BrightFarms is growing it in urban areas near grocery retailers. They partner with the grocers who sign product purchase agreements (PPAs), or in this case "produce" purchase agreements, for up to ten years using a fixed formula. These contracts represent a cash-flow stream that provides confidence for investors who then provide the capital to build the greenhouses. The produce itself might cost more to produce than the industrial farm, but when the reduction in transportation (fuel) expense is factored in, the net price to the grocery store is actually lower than industrial produce. Reducing the supply chain reduces demand for oil, which may eventually cause oil prices to go down.

The benefit is freshly grown food, close to the store. The food is higher quality and healthier for the consumer. The costs are fixed for the grocery store, and there are locally created urban farming jobs. Plus there is increased energy efficiency from the insulating value of the rooftop farm and reduced storm runoff.

Last spring, BrightFarms signed an agreement for a multi-acre farm to be built in Brooklyn, New York, atop an old federal building that is near the waterfront. This is the largest rooftop farm ever built and is being done in conjunction with Mayor Michael Bloomberg's redevelopment project aiming to revitalize the waterfront district.

According to BrightFarms's projections, this rooftop farm will grow enough fresh food to feed five thousand New Yorkers, create jobs, and prevent roughly 1.8 million gallons of storm water from entering local waterways. It was hailed by many, but New York City Council Speaker Christine C. Quinn may have said it best when she said, "The partnership between BrightFarms and Salmar Properties to build the world's largest rooftop farm is an exciting new model for sustainable, urban agriculture."

As is the case when we talk about many solar energy solutions, the technology here for hydroponic farming is not new. There are no new elements to how the food is being raised other than the fact it is being done on a rooftop, which requires a more complex business model to explain to banks and lenders. The key to success here is, like with SunEdison's "solar as a service" model, the grocers are signing extended produce purchase agreements. The "value" created comes from lower transportation costs, leaving room to build in profit margin and still keep prices lower than what would come in from a distant grower.

BrightFarms is one example of how a proven technology, hydroponic gardening, is being deployed using a new business model. This model is helping to jump start hydroponic gardening nationwide with other companies popping up. When an industry has multiple competitors, as we did at SunEdison, it is proof that you are part of building an industry – not just a single company.

This type of innovative thinking is what we are calling for from entrepreneurs worldwide. We need to identify where there are demands and then rethink the current approaches to make completely sure that we maintain a competitive edge, create opportunities for investment and earnings, and solve problems with simple, smart, scalable solutions that we *know* will work.

CHAPTER TWENTY-FIVE:
It Is Up to Us

It is up to us to create a robust economy while solving the issues of climate change—to create climate wealth.

And we all have a part to play. You have a part to play if you are a well-intentioned person looking for a job, an impact investor looking to make an outsized difference, an entrepreneur with a dream, a large corporation with a growth problem, or a government official anxious to figure out how to accelerate deployment of climate solutions.

Today, there are real stories of real people who are playing a part in the creation of climate wealth. You have read about some of them in the preceding pages. It is inspiring because each new business and each person put to work in the climate-wealth economy is overcoming the odds.

Climate-wealth creation is this generation's big inspirational opportunity. But across the Carbon War Room's seventeen sectors displayed in Chapter sixteen we have not yet truly seized the moment.

Solar, which is near and dear to my heart, is an industry where we are seizing the moment.

Here are the facts. In 2012, about one hundred billion dollars of solar was installed around the world. According to John Farrell at the Institute for Local Self Reliance, the average solar project size was about thirty four kW or one hundred thousand dollars. This means that in 2012, there were almost 1 million projects. Across all sectors of clean energy, Bloomberg New Energy Finance estimates that $269 billion was invested in 2012.

The astounding thing about clean energy is that Fortune 500 companies do not dominate this sector. Most of the companies responsible for deploying this money over these projects are less than fifteen years old—including the company I started in January 2003. It is happening at the local level with local entrepreneurs making projects a reality.

In practical terms, the solar industry has started a local revolution—one project at a time, one community at a time, one rooftop at a time. Even now, most of the traditional energy providers have a hard time thinking that these small projects will ever amount to anything at scale, but at $269 billion in 2012, the politicians are open to looking at solar solutions as a source of local economic development.

All Climate Change Solutions Are Local

Thomas "Tip" O'Neill, the infamous speaker of the House of Representatives, wrote *All Politics Is Local*. I suggest that all energy solutions that will build our climate-wealth economy are local as well.

To solve climate change and reach ten trillion dollars in investments by 2020, we have to increase the number of projects and dollars by about thirty five percent per year. At this scale, we need every successful stay-at-home parent, school board member, former city council official, commercial real estate broker, Realtor, Rotary Club member, and others in this field.

Reaching this goal will not necessarily be easy, but it is doable. The lessons around accessing mainstream capital in this book are at the heart of identifying why some succeed and most fail. How can we make certain we chase the right projects—those that reach a successful conclusion?

Across most of the seventeen sectors, the efforts to create climate wealth are deployed at the local level by entrepreneurs. Early risk takers do the business development work to identify local opportunities unpaid until there is a successful project close.

This means choosing the right projects is everything. Today, many know about local opportunities to put solar on schools, but how many are up to speed on vehicle fleet conversions, building efficiency, local agriculture, water efficiency, and other opportunities? We are standing at a moment when the fundamentals of infrastructure can be transformed, and it will be done through an army of local zealots who want to do well financially by doing good.

More Inspirational Visions

In electricity today, incentive programs and renewable portfolio standards have shocked the system. How? Electric utility companies must produce an increasing percent of their electricity generation from renewable sources. The result is that almost 50 percent of new electricity sources in the United States over the past five years have come from wind, solar, geothermal, and other renewable sources.

And because the electricity grid and our coal generating plants are so old, they are going to need to be replaced by something. So what should we replace them with: natural gas? After all, we do have choices.

While natural gas is abundant, does natural gas inspire us? Does it really create a clean energy future? My sense is that very few are inspired by a natural-gas-powered future—it looks too much like the past. It is a centrally distributed fuel source. It is not local.

A more inspirational vision is local energy. Consider that solar power and other local sources of energy will be cost effective without subsidies by 2017; for twenty percent of Americans, ideal solar projects have already achieved this mark. Renewable energy in the United States was forty nine percent of new capacity additions and forty billion dollars of new investments in 2012. With enough local champions, this could move to one hundred percent of new capacity additions and one hundred billion dollars in new investments by 2017. At a typical 2-percent sales commission, there is two billion dollars available to help local champions do well by doing good.

More importantly, every household and business in America can choose to take control of its electricity future. By implementing local electricity production, a home or business can protect itself from ever-increasing electricity prices. Plus, they can add features like reliable power, remote monitoring, and freedom from the dreaded dependence upon the local electric utility company. In other words, citizens have real freedom and individual choice from collective utility decision-making.

This will not happen without at least a hundred thousand local champions identifying projects at the local level that meet the criteria mainstream capital has set for investment.

In terms of oil, the United States has reduced its oil consumption every year for the past seven years. President Obama passed new CAFE standards to double automobile fuel efficiency from its present level by 2025. We will also be drilling a lot more expensive unconventional oil locally. Today's policy direction will ensure that oil prices will stay high for decades to come. But energy independence through high oil prices and increased drilling is not inspirational; it is more of the same.

A more inspirational vision is that by 2020, we ensure that no American is shackled to a car payment again. If you choose to live in an urban or suburban area—as over fifty percent of Americans do—and you want to live without a car payment, we can make that easy and pleasant. We will allow entrepreneurs to implement the infrastructure necessary for convenient car sharing, car renting by the hour, bike sharing, and other measures to make that dream a reality. This will free up public transportation to do more with its existing infrastructure. It can finally take the worst investment a person makes in their entire life, a personal vehicle, off the "to-do" list.

The other fifty percent of Americans who need a car will have a choice— fuel choice. No longer will you have to choose between gasoline and diesel. Consumers now have the technology to force all cars to burn multiple liquid fuels. This means vehicles can fill up on ethanol, methanol, gasoline, and for some cars up to forty five percent natural gas.

Because most homes in America are hooked to both natural gas and electricity, you can also choose an electric car or one hundred-percent natural gas car and fill up at home and work. Further, we can absolutely convert one hundred percent of the fleet vehicles in the United States to natural gas or electricity by 2020. At only two dollars per gallon, natural gas and electricity can diminish the extra five hundred billion dollars per year that Americans pay for gasoline today versus what they paid in 1999. Fuel choice will "future-proof" cars and trucks. Fuel competition would finally provide some chance that we can contain costs.

Again, the only way to reach this goal is for one hundred thousand local champions to convince the city officials and fleet owners to follow all the case studies and convert their vehicles to save money—and make a commission doing it. The oil reduction side is another one hundred billion dollar annual investment opportunity.

As you have read, technologies exist across many sectors, but that's not enough. We need deployment. And that means we need you.

We need people with a penchant for using their networks to influence local decision makers in their community to move these solutions along faster. By doing so, they ensure that their community receives economic development and local job creation.

Government Guidance and Mainstream Capital

While deployment is at the local level, we need guidance and clear signals from mainstream capital and national and state governments. Innovation is very important, yet deployment only happens when local entrepreneurs receive clear signals so they can be sure they are not wasting their time. We need a coordinated effort to provide entrepreneurs the right signals around technologies we have already invented.

As I noted in chapter six, the government's role is critical. I am not talking about government deployment subsidies. The government can help solve our big issues of mobility, energy, and water through steps we discussed: industry coordination, creating a plan—a roadmap—ending subsidies for mature industries and being first-mover users.

The funding for deployment can come from mainstream capital. It is money we are already planning to spend anyway. For example, in the United States, more than seventy seven thousand MW of coal plants could be retired by 2020; replacing this old coal with new coal at today's prices would cost over four hundred billion dollars. That is about the same amount of money to build clean energy plants—except that clean energy plants are deflationary, meaning the price goes down substantially after they are fully paid for because there are not any fuel costs. Another six hundred billion dollars can be spent on energy efficiency, thermal storage, intelligent grid efforts, demand response, and other innovations that will bring us into the twenty-first century.

We have seen this kind of coordination in solar. With mainstream capital funding and government guidance in the form of renewable portfolio standards, deployment subsidies, and net metering, the solar industry has been able to take off. Today, solar can do without the deployment subsidies, as can technologies in many other sectors.

The solar industry grew from one thousand MW of deployment in 2003 to more than thirty thousand MW in 2012—a growth rate of forty-plus percent annually. As Ray Kurzwell has said, exponential growth rates have a way of surprising you. If the solar industry maintains this kind of growth rate, as is predicted, solar will reach two hundred thousand MWs per year by 2020 and four hundred billion dollars in annual investments. With this growth in solar, coupled with similar growth in other renewable energy technologies, we can easily meet one hundred percent of incremental electricity needs globally from zero-emission sources (including efficiency).

This is the kind of exponential growth that can be started across all of the Carbon War Room's industry sectors simply by teaching entrepreneurs how to access mainstream project finance. Entrepreneurs are not naturally educated about mainstream capital—they usually have far more expertise in their technology and core business model. Solar is a proof point. Our final proof will be in deployment. And the creation of climate wealth is ultimately up to each of us.

Jigar Shah

Jigar Shah grew up in Sterling, Illinois, a rural town of about 15,000 due west of Chicago. From that unassuming beginning, Shah became the person who unlocked a multi-billion dollar worldwide solar industry with a business model innovation, not a new technology. This model created SunEdison, the largest solar services company worldwide.

SunEdison did not start from a dream, it started when Jigar read a science book as a teen and learned how solar worked. From that day he asked, "why can't this be everywhere?" It drove him to do something about it. Through SunEdison, Jigar discovered he could make positive change through business and financial model innovation in many industries. Today, as CEO of Jigar Shah Consulting, he works with global companies in a multitude of industries to deploy existing clean energy solutions fueled by new business models.

After SunEdison was sold in 2009, Jigar was appointed the first CEO of the Carbon War Room—the global organization founded by Sir Richard Branson and Virgin Unite to help entrepreneurs address climate change. Carbon War Room, broadened and deepened Jigar's global knowledge of the myriad of business solutions that will build the next economy.

He sits on the boards of the Carbon War Room, SolarNexus KMR Infrastructure, and Empower Energies.

Shah holds a BS in mechanical engineering from the University of Illinois, Champaign-Urbana, and an MBA from The University of Maryland. And Jigar is proud to be an Eagle Scout.

When Jigar is not busy exploring new business solutions for electricity, agriculture, building efficiency, clean transportation and other sectors, he can usually be found exploring new foods, new travels, or spending time with his family.

Jigar lives in New York with his wife, Khushali.

Thank you:

When writing a thank you, your greatest fear is that you will forget someone—I hope it wasn't you! First, I must thank Bill Rever for the countless conversations at BP Solar that gave me the knowledge necessary to start SunEdison. Next, thank you to my SunEdison family, who believed in me when I was only twenty-eight years old and crazily followed me to the ends of the earth. The next thank you goes to Richard Branson for seeing in me a talent that was worth nurturing and bringing to a global stage at the Carbon War Room. To my Carbon War Room family, I hope that through this book you have seen how much you have touched my life, changed my thoughts, and how passionately I believe that we can solve climate change with existing technologies.

Most importantly I want to thank Rob Wyse. Rob saw in me a talent I didn't know I possessed back in 2006, when he was helping me as the CEO of SunEdison. Through all of the years since then, he has continued to believe in me and has never left my side.

Lastly, I want to thank Gayle Dendinger for believing my ideas had merit and a thank you to Bob Weinstein, who helped jumpstart this book, to Kim DeCoste, whose tireless work actually made this book a reality, Jan Mazotti, whose professionalism improved this book substantially, and the rest of the brilliant *ICOSA* team, whose 100-percent support was much appreciated.

Works Cited

Chapter 1

Eberhard, Martin. August 9, 2006. "One Brick at a Time." http://www.teslamotors.com/fr_CA/node/3918. Accessed April 4, 2013.

Chapter 2

FuelFreedom.org. "Oil Economics: The Big Picture." http://www.fuel-freedom.org/the-real-foreign-oil-problem/oil-economics. Accessed December 4, 2012.

Lovins, Amory; Data, E. Kyle; Bustnes, Odd-Even; Koomey, Jonathan G.; Glasgow, Nathan J. *Winning the Oil Endgame: Innovation for Profits, Jobs & Security*. Rocky Mountain Institute. Boulder, Colorado.

Moore, Bill. April 23, 2006. "The Hidden Cost of Our Oil Dependence." http://www.benzworld.org/forums/off-topic/1260216-hidden-cost-our-oil-dependence.html. Accessed December 19, 2012.

Wald, Mathew. October 19, 2009. "Fossil Fuels Hidden Cost Is in Billions, Study Says." *New York Times*. Accessed November 14, 2012.

Napach, Denise. January 29, 2013. "U.S. Still Suffering Depression Conditions: Paul Krugman." *Yahoo! Finance: The Daily Ticker*. Accessed January 29, 2013.

Minkel, JR. August 13, 2008. "The 2003 Northeast Blackout—Five Years Later." *Scientific American*. Accessed November 7, 2012.

Chapter 4

Say, Jean-Baptiste. 1855. *A Treatise on Political Economy*. Lippencot, Grambo & Co. Philadelphia.

SBA.gov. 2013. "What Is an Entrepreneur?" http://www.sba.gov/content/what-entrepreneur. Accessed January 20, 2013.

Ash, Roy. http://thinkexist.com/quotation/an_entrepreneur_tends_to_bite_off_a_little_more/252632.html. Accessed January 19, 2013.

Ferris, Tim. "Escaping the Entrepreneurial Seizure: Interview with Michael Gerber (Plus: Tim Speaking)." February 27, 2008. http://www.fourhourworkweek.com/blog/2008/02/27/escaping-the-entrepreneurial-seizure-interview-with-michael-gerber-plus-tim-speaking/. Accessed January 19, 2013.

Hagedoorn, John. 1985. "Innovation and Entrepreneurship: Schumpeter Revisited." PDF retrieved online, Maastricht University, The Netherlands. Accessed January 15, 2013.

Skok, David. June 12, 2010. "What Drives Great Entrepreneurs?" http://www.forentrepreneurs.com/what-drives-great-entrepreneurs . Accessed January 16, 2013.

Chapter 5

Awerbach, Shimon; Yang, Spencer. "An Efficient, Sustainable and Secure Supply of Energy for Europe." *EIB Papers*. Volume 12. Number 2, 2007. Accessed online February 12, 2013.

Sittampalam, Dr. Arjuna. May 16, 2011. "Impact Investing versus Socially Responsible Investing." EDHEC-RISK Institute. http://www.edhec-risk.com/latest_news/featured_analysis/RISKArticle.2011-05-16.5902?newsletter=yes. Accessed August 29, 2011.

Chapter 7

Gladwell, Malcolm. 2000. *The Tipping Point: How Little Things Can Make a Big Difference*. Bay Back Books. New York, New York.

Chapter 8

Taleb, Nassim Nicholas. 2001. *Fooled by Randomness: The Hidden Role of Chance in Life and in the Markets.* Random House. London.

Cohen, Jason. March 30, 2009. "How Much of Success Is Luck?" http://blog.asmartbear.com/how-much-of-success-is-luck.html . Accessed November 13, 2012.

O'Loughlin, James. 2003. *The Real Warren Buffett: Managing Capital, Leading People.* Nicholas Brealey Publishing. Boston, Massachusetts.

Chapter 12

Rosengren, Curt. July 10, 2008. "Do What You Love But Money Won't Necessarily Follow." http://money.usnews.com/money/blogs/outside-voices-careers/2008/07/10/do-what-you-love-but-money-wont-necessarily-follow. Accessed December 2, 2012.

Kawasaki, Guy. February 18, 2007. "Make Meaning in Your Company—Guy Kawasaki from Garage Technology Ventures." http://pr-lead.com/make-meaning-in-your-company-guy-kawasaki-from-garage-technology-ventures. Accessed November 9, 2012.

Chapter 14

Casey, Paul E. 2004. *Is Self-Employment for You? Anyone Can Start a Business…Only a Few Can Sustain a Business.* Hara Publishing Group. Bothell, Washington.

Chapter 15

Hewicker, Christian; Hogan, Michael; Mogren, Arne. October 2009. *Power Perspective 2030: On the Road to a Decarbonized Power Sector.* DNV KIM A & The European Climate Foundation.

Chapter 17

Hand, Dr. Maureen, and Trieu, Dr. Mai. June 12, 2012. "Renewable Electricity Futures." National Renewable Energy Labs (NREL) Publication. PDF accessed online January 4, 2013.

Chapter 18

Pope, Carl. January 4, 2012. "Solar Power Off the Grid: Energy Access for the World's Poor." http://e360.yale.edu/feature/solar_power_off_the_grid_energy_access_for_worlds_poor/2480. Accessed January 7, 2013.

International Energy Agency. World Energy Outlook. "Energy for All: Financing Access for the Poor." http://www.iea.org/publications/freepublications/publication/weo2011_energy_for_all.pdf. Accessed January 7, 2013.

Made in the USA
San Bernardino, CA
20 October 2013